CROCHET
from the
HEART

QUICK PROJECTS FOR GENEROUS GIVING

Kristin Spurkland

Martingale®
& COMPANY

Acknowledgments

Thank you to everyone who helped me create this book: Sandy Bingham for testing the Footies pattern and for continually sharing her good ideas with me; Jamie Guinn for doing such a fantastic job lining the Rainbow Baby Blanket; and all my friends in the knitting and crochet community and at House of Dreams for their continued support and encouragement.

Thank you, Brent. Your photos are fabulous!

Thank you to my family for believing in me.

Thank you, Toady!

Credits

President ♥ Nancy J. Martin

CEO ♥ Daniel J. Martin

VP and General Manager ♥ Tom Wierzbicki

Publisher ♥ Jane Hamada

Editorial Director ♥ Mary V. Green

Managing Editor ♥ Tina Cook

Technical Editor ♥ Ursula Reikes

Copy Editor ♥ Liz McGehee

Design Director ♥ Stan Green

Illustrator ♥ Laurel Strand

Cover Designer ♥ Stan Green

Text Designer ♥ Regina Girard

Photographer ♥ Brent Kane

Photo Stylist ♥ Kristin Spurkland

Crochet from the Heart:
Quick Projects for Generous Giving
© 2005 by Kristin Spurkland

Martingale & Company
20205 144th Avenue NE
Woodinville, WA 98072-8478 USA
www.martingale-pub.com

Printed in China
10 09 08 07 06 05   8 7 6 5 4 3 2 1

Mission Statement

Dedicated to providing quality products and service to inspire creativity.

Library of Congress Cataloging-in-Publication Data
Spurkland, Kristin.
   Crochet from the heart : quick projects for generous giving / Kristin Spurkland.
      p. cm.
   ISBN 1-56477-606-9
   1. Crocheting—Patterns. I. Title.
   TT825.S 7134 2005
   746.43'4041—dc22

                              2005012747

CONTENTS

6   Introduction

7   Crochet Techniques

19   Finishing

The Projects

22   Rainbow Baby Blanket

25   Sweet Baby Hat

28   Booties

31   Pretty Baby Blanket

33   Pretty Pink Hat and Scarf

36   Finger Puppets

40   Flowers

44   Floral Wristbands and Choker

47   Classic Hat

50   Fingerless Mitts

52   Footies

56   Kitty's Bed

59   Ruffle-Edge Hat

62   Color-Block Scarves

65   Lap Blanket

68   Retro Scarf

71   Geometric Bags

74   Preemie Hats

77   Useful Information

78   Charitable Organizations

80   About the Author

INTRODUCTION

The theme of my first book, *Knits from the Heart: Quick Projects for Generous Giving,* is all about sharing our talents for knitting with those around us, be it our friends and family or the family at the local emergency shelter. I am pleased to now offer another book in the same theme, but this time for those of you who crochet.

The publication of *Knits from the Heart* introduced me to people from around the country—people who called or emailed me to tell me about what they do to help those in need in their communities. These inspiring and uplifting conversations confirm my own experience: community service makes a difference in the lives of not only the population receiving the service, but in the lives of the givers as well.

With this book, I invite you to share your crochet skills with others—both those in your immediate circle, and those you may have never met but who will appreciate your gifts all the same. Crochet hats can be given to hospitals to share with premature babies or patients undergoing chemotherapy. Hats, mittens, socks, and scarves are needed at homeless shelters, and blankets can give comfort to children going through illness or family crisis. There are countless ways to use your crochet skills to benefit your community. If you need some more ideas, consult the index in the back of this book for information on organizations that accept crochet donations.

If you're going to donate a handmade item, please remember that easy-care yarns are usually best. You don't want your lovely crochet cap to be ruined in the wash! If you're unsure, contact the organization you're donating to and ask them for their preferences.

CROCHET TECHNIQUES

Take a minute to familiarize yourself with the following how-to information. It's here for a reason: to provide answers to common questions and help you when you're stuck or confused. If you find yourself stumped by a technique or instruction in a pattern, return to this section and see if you can't find the explanation you need.

When learning these techniques, it's best to work with the yarn and hook in your hands, following the instructions step by step as you read. Just reading the instructions, without actually trying the technique, can be a thoroughly confusing experience. So get out that hook and get crocheting!

Holding the Hook

The most common ways to hold the hook are either like a pencil or like a knife. Experiment to find the method that works best for you. And if you come up with a new way of holding the hook, that's OK too, as long as you can make the stitches easily and comfortably.

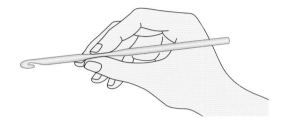

Hold like a pencil

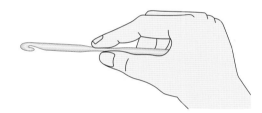

Hold like a knife

Holding the Yarn

Just as there is more than one way to hold the hook, there are many ways to hold the yarn. The main thing is to maintain enough tension on the yarn to easily form the stitches. Most people work with the yarn over their index finger, with the thumb and middle finger lightly holding their work. You can experiment with wrapping the yarn around your index finger or your other fingers to control the tension. Play around until you find the way that works best for you.

A Note to Lefties

If you're left-handed, you can try crocheting as right-handed people do, with the hook in your right hand and your yarn in your left. If you prefer, go ahead and try crocheting left-handed, with the hook in your left hand and your yarn in your right. If you're learning from another (right-handed) crocheter, sit across from her and mirror her movements. You also may want to seek out directions geared specifically for lefties.

Using Markers

When I was learning to crochet, I put markers in everything—the tops of chains, the bases of chains, the first stitch of the row, the slip stitch joining one round to another. Everything got a marker (I used different colors to mark different areas), and before long I could recognize the various elements of crochet fabric without having to mark them. When learning a new stitch pattern, I still use markers to keep me on track. It's the best method I've found for keeping things clear and understandable.

Use split-ring markers when you crochet, as they allow you to remove and replace the markers with each subsequent row or round.

Making the Base Chain

Crochet projects usually begin with a base chain (also called a foundation chain). Before making your base chain, you have to attach the yarn to the hook, usually by means of a slip knot. An alternative to the slip knot is the technique "Simple Start," explained below. The two techniques are interchangeable, so use whichever you like best.

Slip Knot

Make a loop with the yarn, leaving about a 6" tail, with the ball end of the yarn away from you. Reach through the loop, grab the ball end of the yarn, and pull the yarn through the loop. Insert the hook through this new loop and tighten the loop down on the hook.

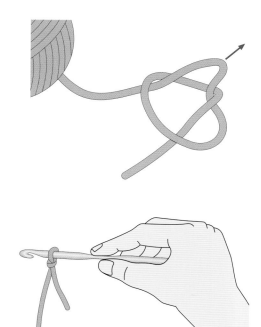

Simple Start

This start is very discreet and, unlike the slip knot, does not leave a knot at the start of the work. I learned this start from one of Elizabeth Zimmerman's books. It works well for hats and other projects that begin with rings (see "Working in Rounds" on page 15), because there is no knot to interfere with pulling the ring tight.

Leaving about a 6" tail, hold the yarn taut over your thumb and index finger, with the ball end of the yarn away from you. Place your hook on top of the taut yarn.

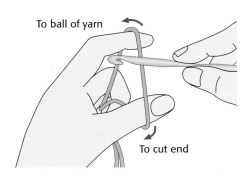

To ball of yarn

To cut end

Rotate your wrist and hand, moving the hook end down, toward your body, under the cut end, and then up and away from you. This motion will wrap the yarn around the hook.

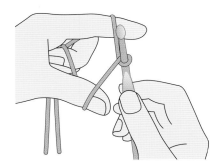

At this point, the only thing keeping the yarn looped around the needle is the tension you put on it with your hands. You have to make a quick and dexterous transition to your first chain stitch to fully secure the yarn. You will need to release the tension a bit and open up the loop on the hook with your fingers in order to make the first chain. This may feel awkward initially, but with practice it will become a cinch.

Wrapping the Yarn over the Hook: Yarn Over (YO)

With hook and yarn in position, wrap the yarn over the top of the hook, from back to front and right to left, catching the yarn in the groove of the hook.

Crocheting a Chain

Make a slip knot or use the technique "Simple Start" (the slip knot/simple start anchors the yarn to the hook and does not count as a chain stitch).

Yarn over, draw the yarn through the slip knot, letting the slip knot slide off the hook. *Yarn over, draw the yarn through the new loop, letting the loop slide off the hook. Repeat from * for the desired number of chains.

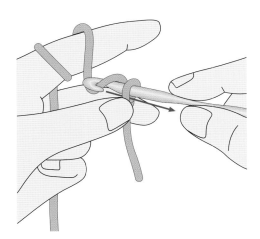

Your chain stitches will look like a string of Vs hanging from your hook. To count your chain stitches, count all the Vs, remembering that the starting slip knot and the loop on the hook are not counted.

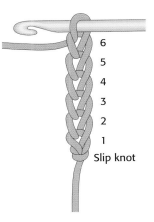

6
5
4
3
2
1
Slip knot

When crocheting a long base chain at the start of a project, placing markers every 20 to 25 chains will help track your progress. You can also make a few extra chains, because any unneeded chains can just be unraveled after working your first row. It's far better to unravel a few extra chain stitches than to find you didn't chain enough and have to start all over!

Crocheting the First Row

When crocheting the first row into the base chain, you can insert the hook under both legs of the chain stitch (the V) or under just one. I find it infinitely easier to work under the top leg only, and the final result is just as nice as if you worked under both.

After the first row, insert the hook under both legs of the stitch, unless instructed otherwise.

Making a Turning Chain

Most crochet patterns will indicate that you work a specific number of chain stitches at the beginning of a row. This chain is called the turning chain (abbreviated in directions as *tch*), and it lifts the hook to the appropriate height for the stitch you're about to work.

The height of the turning chain (and the number of chains in the turning chain) is determined by the stitch pattern you're crocheting. Single crochet gets 1 chain, half double crochet gets 2 chains, and double crochet gets 3 chains. Most patterns will include this information, so you don't have to memorize it.

Make a turning chain as follows: When you get to the end of the row, turn your work, chain the

number of stitches indicated, and proceed with the pattern.

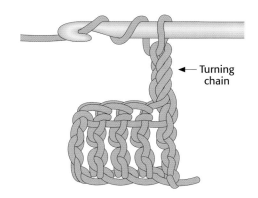

The turning chain in single crochet is never counted as a stitch. However, the turning chain in half double crochet and double crochet is sometimes counted as the first stitch of the row, sometimes not. When the turning chain is counted as a stitch, the selvages of the crocheted piece are straighter. So when working a project such as a scarf or a blanket that won't have any borders added, counting the turning chain as a stitch keeps the edges tidy. When the turning chain isn't counted, the chain curves out a bit, creating a slight scallop along the selvage. You can use this scallop for seaming, for picking up stitches for borders, or as a decorative element.

How will you know if the turning chain is being counted as a stitch? If the instructions tell you to work the last stitch of the row into the top of the turning chain from the previous row, then the chain is probably being counted as a stitch. When you see the direction, for example, "rep from * to last 2 sts, sk 1 st, dc in top of tch," the turning chain from the previous row will be the last of the 2 stitches in the row. If you don't work into the top of the previous row's turning chain, then the turning chain is probably not being counted.

Don't worry too much about this rule if you're a beginner. Just follow the instructions as written, and eventually you will learn to distinguish between counting and not counting the turning chain.

Using a Double Chain (dbl ch)

The double-chain technique creates a base chain followed by a row of single crochet all in one shot, saving you the step of having to work a row of single crochet on a long, snaky chain. I like to use it for patterns requiring a long base chain, as the extra stability makes the first row easier to work.

Chain 2, insert hook in second chain from hook, yarn over, draw yarn through chain (2 loops on hook), yarn over, draw yarn through both loops. *Insert hook in left loop of single crochet just made, yarn over (fig. 1), draw yarn through left loop only (2 loops on hook; fig. 2), yarn over, draw yarn through both loops (fig. 3). Repeat from * for the desired number of chains.

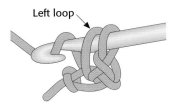

Left loop

Fig. 1

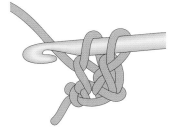

Fig. 2

Fig. 3

If you use a double chain on a pattern that does not call for it specifically, and the first row of the pattern is in single crochet, omit that first single-crochet row, because the double chain replicates a regular base chain followed by a row of single crochet.

Take a look at your chain. Down one side there are a series of Vs similar to what you see after making a regular chain. Down the other are a series of single loops. When working the first row after making a double chain, work under these single loops. The Vs become the lower edge of your fabric, giving it a finished look without having to add any additional border or edging.

Reading Crochet Instructions

In order to follow written crochet instructions, it is important to understand the following terms.

First Stitch

If you're working flat (in rows), the first stitch of the row is the stitch the turning chain emerges from. See "Working in Rounds" on page 15 for information on determining the first stitch on in-the-round projects.

Next Stitch

The next stitch is the stitch immediately following the stitch you just worked into. Example: "sc in next st, dc in next st, sc in next st" means single crochet in the next available stitch, double crochet in the stitch after that, and single crochet in the stitch after that. The above instructions *are not* telling you to work all three stitches into a single stitch. Those instructions would read "(sc, dc, sc) in next st."

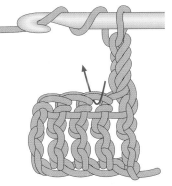

Next stitch

Base of Turning Chain

The stitch the turning chain emerges from is the base of the turning chain. When crocheting flat, this is the same as the first stitch of the row. When crocheting in rounds, it may or may not be the same as the first stitch (see "Working in Rounds" on page 15).

Top of Turning Chain

The final chain of the turning chain is the top of the turning chain. Patterns will often instruct you to work the last stitch of a row into the top of the turning chain of the previous row. Placing a marker in the top of the turning chain makes it much easier to locate.

Turn

Turn your work around to start the next row. Turn the same way every time, either clockwise or counterclockwise, to avoid distorting the edges of your fabric.

Work Even

Continue in the established stitch pattern, without any increases or decreases.

Learning the Basic Stitches

The following basic crochet stitches form the foundation of many other stitch patterns.

Slip Stitch (sl st)

The slip stitch is unusual in that it does not require a turning chain. It is primarily used to finish edges or to join one round to another when making circular items like hats.

In the base chain: Insert hook in second chain from hook, yarn over, draw yarn through both

loops. *Insert hook in next chain, yarn over, draw yarn through both loops. Repeat from *.

On the rows that follow: Insert hook in first st, yarn over, draw yarn through both loops. *Insert hook in next stitch, yarn over, draw yarn through both loops. Repeat from *.

Single Crochet (sc)

In the base chain: Insert hook in second chain from hook, yarn over, draw yarn through this chain only (2 loops on hook; fig. 4), yarn over, draw yarn through both loops (fig. 5). *Insert hook in next chain, yarn over, draw yarn through this chain only (2 loops on hook), yarn over, draw yarn through both loops. Repeat from *.

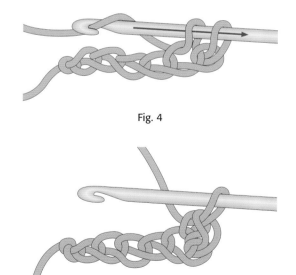

Fig. 4

Fig. 5

On the rows that follow: Chain 1, insert hook in first stitch, yarn over, draw yarn through this stitch only (2 loops on hook), yarn over, draw yarn through both loops. *Insert hook in next stitch, yarn over, draw yarn through this stitch only (2 loops on hook), yarn over, draw yarn through both loops. Repeat from *.

Half Double Crochet (hdc)

In the base chain: Yarn over, insert hook in third chain from hook, yarn over, draw yarn through this chain only (3 loops on hook; fig. 6), yarn over, draw yarn through all 3 loops (fig. 7). *Yarn over, insert hook in next chain, yarn over, draw yarn through this chain only (3 loops on hook), yarn over, draw yarn through all 3 loops. Repeat from *.

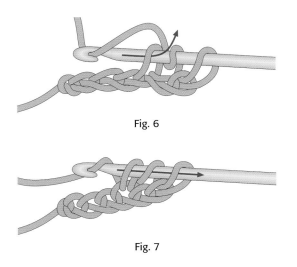

Fig. 6

Fig. 7

On the rows that follow: Chain 2, yarn over, insert hook in second stitch, yarn over, draw yarn through this stitch only (3 loops on hook), yarn over, draw through all 3 loops. *Yarn over, insert hook in next stitch, yarn over, draw yarn through this stitch only (3 loops on hook), yarn over, draw yarn through all 3 loops. Repeat from *. At the end of the row, work 1 half double crochet in top of turning chain.

Double Crochet (dc)

In the base chain: Yarn over, insert hook in fourth chain from hook (fig. 8), yarn over, draw yarn through this chain only (3 loops on hook), yarn over, draw yarn through first 2 loops on hook (2 loops on hook; fig. 9), yarn over, draw yarn through

remaining 2 loops (fig. 10). *Yarn over, insert hook in next chain, yarn over, draw yarn through this chain only (3 loops on hook), yarn over, draw yarn through first 2 loops on hook (2 loops on hook), yarn over, draw yarn through remaining 2 loops. Repeat from *.

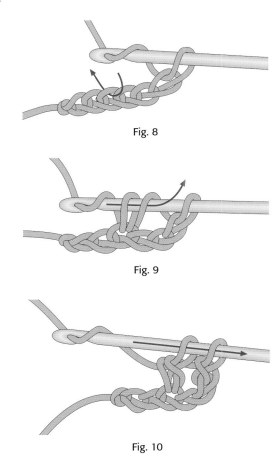

Fig. 8

Fig. 9

Fig. 10

On the rows that follow: Chain 3, yarn over, insert hook in second stitch, yarn over, draw yarn through this stitch only (3 loops on hook), yarn over, draw yarn through first 2 loops on hook (2 loops on hook), yarn over, draw yarn through remaining 2 loops. *Yarn over, insert hook in next stitch, yarn over, draw yarn through this stitch only (3 loops on hook), yarn over, draw yarn through first 2 loops on hook (2 loops on hook), yarn over, draw yarn through remaining 2 loops. Repeat from *. At the end of the row, work 1 double crochet in top of turning chain.

Working into the Front Loop Only (flo) or Back Loop Only (blo) of a Stitch

Work your stitch as usual, inserting your hook under only the front leg ("front loop") or the back leg ("back loop") of the stitch from the previous row. This technique can be applied to any stitch. It creates horizontal ridges across your work and usually creates a softer, more fluid fabric.

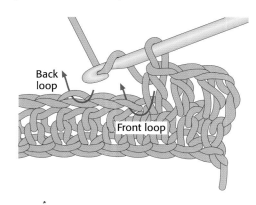

Increasing

Work 2 (or more) stitches in the next stitch. Your pattern will tell you exactly when and how many stitches to increase.

Decreasing

In single crochet: Insert hook in next stitch, yarn over, draw yarn through this stitch only (2 loops on hook), insert hook in next stitch, yarn over, draw yarn through this stitch only (3 loops on hook), yarn over, draw yarn through all 3 loops.

In double crochet: Yarn over, insert hook in next stitch, yarn over, draw yarn through this stitch only (3 loops on hook), yarn over, draw yarn through first 2 loops on hook (2 loops on hook; fig. 11), yarn over, insert hook in next stitch, yarn over, draw yarn through this stitch only (4 loops on hook; fig. 12), yarn over, draw yarn through first 2 loops on hook (3 loops on hook; fig. 13), yarn over, and draw yarn through remaining 3 loops (fig. 14).

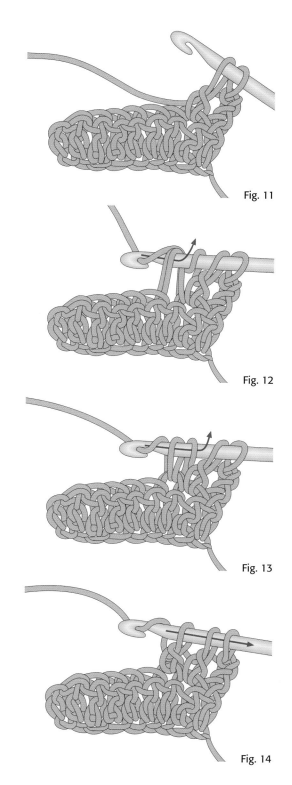

Fig. 11

Fig. 12

Fig. 13

Fig. 14

Grasp the concept behind decreasing and you can decrease in any stitch pattern. It's really very simple: Work the first of the decrease stitches as usual, stopping just before the final yarn over.

Leave the remaining loops on the hook. Work the next stitch, drawing the final yarn over through all the loops on the hook, including those remaining from the first stitch.

Working in Rounds

Working in rounds allows you to crochet a circular or cylindrical fabric without any seams. The projects Footies, Kitty's Bed, and all the hats in this book are worked in rounds, and the ubiquitous Granny Square is a classic in-the-round project.

There are two ways of starting a project worked in rounds: the ring start and the chain start. Patterns in this book state which start I used; however, once you understand each start, you can interchange them as you prefer.

Ring Start

This is the most common way to start a circular project. Make a chain (your pattern will tell you how long to make it). Join the last chain to the first chain with a slip stitch, forming the chain into a ring.

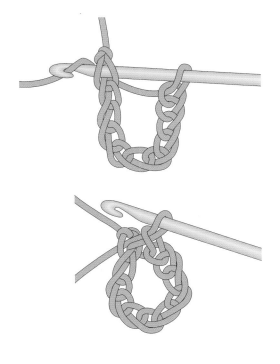

Your next round will have you working stitches "into the ring." This means that you insert your hook in the center of the ring (rather than under the legs of the chains) when forming your first round of stitches.

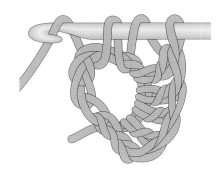

Chain Start

I used single crochet in the example below; however, you can use this start for any stitch pattern, adjusting the number of stitches worked into the chain according to the pattern specifications.

Chain 2, work 6 single crochets in second chain from hook (fig. 15). Place a marker in the first single crochet made, do not turn (fig. 16). Work 2 single crochets in the marked stitch (this will join work into a circle) and 2 single crochets in the next 5 stitches. You should now have 12 stitches and the beginning of a flat circle.

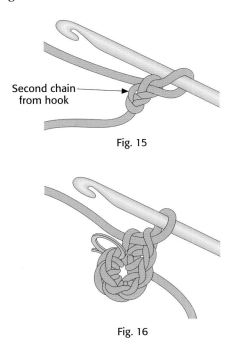

Second chain from hook

Fig. 15

Fig. 16

The number of stitches you work into the chain will vary with the stitch pattern used, as will the number of chains you start with. The example on page 15 is just to give you an idea of how this start works.

Concentric vs. Spiral Shaping

There are two ways to work projects in the round: concentric or spiral shaping. Each one has its advantages and disadvantages, and I have used both techniques in this book.

When working in concentric rings, the last stitch of the round is joined to the first stitch of the round with a slip stitch. A chain is worked to lift the hook to the height of the next round. Each round stacks on top of the previous round. Remember the child's toy with the brightly colored plastic "doughnuts" in progressively larger sizes that were stacked on a spindle? That's the same concept. This means that there is no "jog" (break in pattern) where one round ends and another begins. The down side is that there is almost always a noticeable "seam" that runs at a slight diagonal along the line of the chains that start each round.

With spiral shaping, you make a continuous coil, with no distinguishable start and end to the rounds. Rounds are not joined with a slip stitch, and there are no chains. So there is no "seam," but there is a noticeable jog between rounds when working in patterns other than single crochet (a short stitch, so it creates a minimal jog). A project worked in double crochet and spiral construction could have an inch or more height difference between the start and end of the round. Think of the spiral of a snail shell to visualize this effect.

I use the spiral construction for single-crochet projects, since it eliminates the seam and is easy to work. But for any other stitch pattern, concentric construction is usually more appropriate.

Finding the First Stitch of the Round

The first stitch of the round is an elusive creature, as its location depends on which type of shaping you're using.

When working flat, the first stitch of the row is the stitch the turning chain emerges from. When working in concentric circles, however, the chain emerges not from the first stitch of the round, but from the slip stitch joining the last stitch to the top of the turning chain. So there is a distinction between the base of the chain and the first stitch of the round. (When working flat, they are the same thing).

With spiral shaping, you have no chain and no slip stitch, and the first stitch of the round is indistinguishable unless you mark it. This marker must be moved into the first stitch of each successive round.

Joining Yarn

The same technique is used both for changing colors and for adding a new skein of yarn when the old one runs out. This can be done in the middle of a row or at a finished edge.

Joining Yarn in the Middle of a Row

Work the last stitch of the old yarn to the final yarn over, and drop the old yarn; then work the final yarn over and complete the stitch with the new yarn. Make sure to leave sufficiently long tails of each color to be able to weave them in easily.

Note that when changing colors, the change actually happens on the last yarn over of the stitch before the color change. If a pattern tells you to work 3 stitches with color A, then 3 stitches with color B, you actually change colors on the last yarn over of the last stitch in A. This leaves you in position to work the next stitch with B.

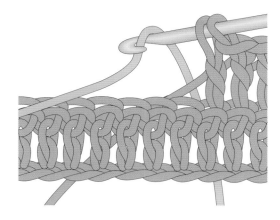

Joining Yarn on a Finished Edge

Sometimes you have to add yarn to a finished edge, meaning there is no "live" stitch to work into. One option is to make a slip knot on your hook with the new yarn, insert your hook in the first stitch to be worked, then proceed as instructed in your pattern.

I don't care for this technique, as it leaves me with a slip knot in the middle of my work that I then have to hide. I prefer to simply insert my hook in the stitch *before* the first stitch to be worked, catch the new yarn with the hook, and draw a loop through the stitch. This gets the new yarn anchored to the fabric and in position to work the first stitch, without the use of any knots.

The initial step of inserting the hook in a stitch, hooking the yarn, and drawing it through does not count as a stitch. It's a set-up step that anchors the yarn. The first stitch is the stitch following this set-up step.

This is all very straightforward when working flat. When working in the round, it's a bit more subtle. Just remember that the last stitch of the round will be worked into the set-up stitch, identifiable by the yarn tail hanging from it. Confused? Count your stitches at the end of your first round with the new yarn, and as long as you have the correct number, you're in business!

Fastening Off

Cut yarn, leaving a tail about 6" long. Pull tail through last stitch and tighten down.

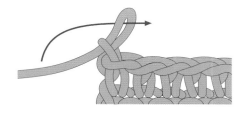

Working with Two or More Colors

You can create interesting effects by using 2 or more colors alternately across a row. Both colors are carried along the back side of the work (rather than cut and rejoined with each color change); you simply switch from one color to the other as your pattern indicates (see "Joining Yarn" above).

The yarn not in use is carried or "stranded" across the back of the work. If a yarn must be stranded for more than 1", it is best to tack it down to the inside of the fabric, as overly long strands run the risk of snagging. To catch the stranded yarn, insert the hook in the next stitch and under the stranded yarn, then form the stitch as usual with the working yarn.

When working with 2 colors, place the main color skein on your right side and the contrast color skein on your left. When you're ready to crochet with the contrast color, pick it up from under the main color. When switching back to the main color, take it from above the contrast color. Working this way will prevent the 2 skeins from twisting, saving you the frustration of untangling your skeins every few rows, and the wrong side of your work will be tidier.

Making a Gauge Swatch

Gauge tells you how many stitches and how many rows make up 1" with your given pattern, hook, and yarn. If you don't have the correct gauge, your hat, sock, or baby bootie isn't going to fit. Therefore, it is imperative that you do a gauge swatch, especially if you use a different yarn than the one specified in the pattern.

In order to get an accurate swatch, you must crochet it with the yarn, hook, and stitch pattern that you will be using for your project. Chain the number of stitches equal to approximately 4". So, if your pattern gives a gauge of 22 stitches and 28 rows to 4", you would chain 22 stitches (plus extra for any skipped stitches at the start of the chain). I like to chain a few extra stitches, to accommodate any pattern repeats. Any extra chains will just hang off the end of your swatch, so there is no danger in chaining too many stitches. For our example, I would chain about 30 stitches. Using the suggested hook size and the stitch pattern required for the project, crochet in pattern until your swatch is about 4" long. Break yarn and fasten off.

Before I measure my swatch, I like to block it in the same manner that the final garment will be blocked. Although it takes some extra time, this step is worth doing, as some patterns change significantly after blocking. If you have the time, wash and dry your swatch in the same manner that you will be washing and drying the finished item. An added benefit of this step is you find out about any potential washing problems (shrinkage, bleeding colors, and so on) prior to making your project.

After blocking your swatch, lay it on a flat surface and measure how many stitches and rows there are to 4". Divide the number of stitches by 4 to find out the number of stitches and rows per inch you're getting with the yarn and hook you're using.

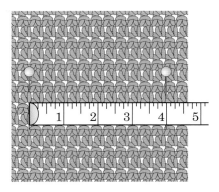

Measuring stitches

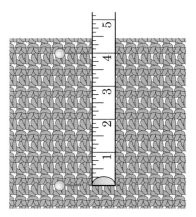

Measuring rows

If you have too many stitches per inch (for example, the pattern says you should have 5½ stitches, but you're counting 6), your stitches are too small and you need to try again on a larger hook. If you have too few stitches (you're only getting 5 stitches to the inch, not the 5½ required), your stitches are too big and you need to use a smaller hook. And yes, fractions of a stitch do matter!

Substituting Yarn

For most of the projects in *Crochet from the Heart*, I have used a hook larger than the one recommended on the yarn label because my stitches tend to be small. If you're going to substitute any of the yarns used in this book, match the weight of the yarn, not the hook size on the yarn label. If I used a DK-weight yarn and an I/9 (5.5 mm) hook, look for another DK-weight yarn, not a yarn that recommends an I/9 hook.

FINISHING

Attention to finishing details will give your work a professional look.

Blocking

Blocking is simply a way of helping your crochet find its proper size and shape through the use of water or steam. Blocking also helps to smooth out any irregularities in texture and tension.

To wet block, wash the item just as you would normally, then lay it out flat on towels and gently coax it into shape. Gentle is the operative word here; you never want to pull roughly on your needlework. Grab a tape measure and your pattern instructions, and shape the piece to the dimensions given in the pattern. Then wait patiently for it to dry. If you remove your work when it is still damp, it may very well revert to its original, pre-blocked shape.

For many projects, a simple steam blocking is sufficient. To steam block, place your project on a covered surface (an ironing board for a small item, a table covered with a towel for larger items), turn your iron to a steam setting, and have your tape measure and pattern within reach. Hold the steam iron an inch or so over your project—direct contact may melt, scorch, or otherwise damage it!—and let the steam permeate the fabric. Shape your project to the size given in the pattern, then wait until it is completely cool and dry before moving it.

Note that steaming may not be appropriate for acrylic and other man-made fibers, as some of them may scorch. If you're unsure, use your swatch as a test piece before steaming your project.

Seaming

There are a number of ways to sew your crochet pieces together. My recommendation is that you use whatever technique works best for you, even if it is something you make up yourself. Here are a couple of techniques I like.

Slip-Stitch Seam

Place pieces to be seamed right sides together. Using your project yarn, *insert hook in both edge stitches, yarn over, draw yarn through stitches and loop on hook. Repeat from * to end of seam.

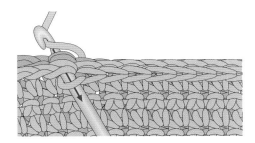

Worked with wrong sides together, this seam creates a small ridge on the right side of the work that can be an attractive design detail.

Overcast Seam

This seam is attractive, fast, and simple to do. I use it more than any other seaming technique. Lay pieces to be seamed side by side, right sides up. With project yarn threaded through a tapestry needle, *insert the needle in the back loop of the edge stitch from each piece, pull the yarn through; repeat from * to end of seam.

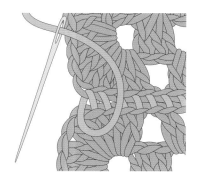

Weaving in Ends

Thread the yarn end through a tapestry needle, and weave the yarn through several stitches on the wrong side of the work. Weave the ends for about 1½" for most items, a little longer for items that will be machine washed and dried or receive heavy use. Check that the ends are not showing on the outside, and cut the yarn.

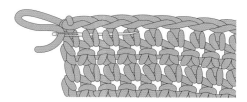

Ending Your Work with a Duplicate-Stitch Join

This technique, based on the duplicate stitch used in knitting, was created because I didn't like the look of the usual method of finishing in-the-round projects (joining the last stitch of the round to the first stitch of the round with a slip stitch).

After working the final stitch of your project, break the yarn and fasten off. Omit the step of joining the last stitch of the round to the first stitch of the round with a slip stitch if your pattern instructs you to do this. Thread the tail through a tapestry needle. Insert the needle from front to back under the legs of the second stitch of the round, then from front to back under the back leg of the last

stitch of the round. You're covering (duplicating) the first stitch of the round. Weave in the tail on the wrong side of your work.

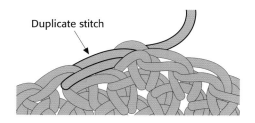

Duplicate stitch

Adding Borders and Edgings

One of the advantages crochet has over knitting is that crochet pieces are often "self-finishing," meaning that they lie flat and look complete without any border added. But sometimes additional finishing is desirable. Often, this will be a row or round of single crochet, perhaps followed by a pattern stitch that creates a ruffle, scallop, or picot.

Crochet directions for borders and edgings frequently say something like "Work single crochet evenly around the blanket," without any specific information about how many stitches to work along each edge. How is it possible to just "work evenly" around an edge and have the edge come out nicely?

Here's how: Crochet stitches accommodate themselves to fit the edge being worked. The loop linking one crochet stitch to another will be longer or shorter according to the distance between the stitches. Two different crocheters making the same project may crochet different numbers of stitches around their respective projects, yet both projects will be successfully finished. Amazing!

My directions generally call for working one edge stitch for each row along side selvages, and one edge stitch for each chain stitch or pattern stitch on the bottom and top edges. I find that this is the simplest and most effective way to edge a project.

The exception to this free-form rule is if you're working an edging that requires a certain number of stitches for a pattern repeat. For example, if you were to add a scallop or shell-stitch edging to a blanket, you would need a specific multiple of stitches in order for the pattern to work. In this case, the pattern would specify how many stitches to work along each edge, and you must work that exact number of stitches to have your pattern come out correctly.

Lining a Blanket

Why should you line a blanket? In addition to adding an interesting design element, linings hide decidedly "wrong" sides of blankets, making an otherwise one-sided blanket reversible. Linings also add warmth and help prevent little fingers from finding their way into the fabric and pulling out stitches. Although it takes a little more time, lining is simple to do and well worth the extra effort.

Always preshrink the fabric you're using to line the blanket; then cut the fabric to the size indicated in the pattern. If you have a serger, serge the edges. If you don't have a serger, don't worry about it; serging makes the job a little easier, but isn't a necessity. Fold fabric edges under ½" all the way around. Pin the fabric to the wrong side of the blanket and hand stitch it into place, using a sewing needle and thread.

Adding French Knots

An embroidery technique, French knots are used to create the faces on the finger puppets (page 36). Thread yarn through a tapestry needle and bring the needle up through the fabric from the wrong side. Holding the yarn taut with your left hand, wrap the yarn around the needle twice (wrap more times for a larger knot; fig. 17). Maintaining the tension on the yarn, reinsert the tapestry needle through the fabric near the place where it originally emerged (fig. 18). Pull the yarn and needle through, making sure to hold the yarn taut throughout (fig. 19). I like to knot the yarn ends on the inside of the fabric when making French knots, to avoid the possibility of them being pulled out.

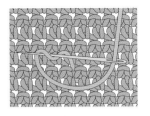

Fig. 17

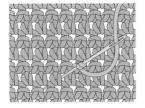

Fig. 18

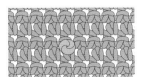

Fig. 19

Making Embroidered Flowers

These sweet little flowers are shown on the Ruffle-Edge Hat (page 59), but you can add them to any of your projects.

Thread yarn through a tapestry needle and *bring needle up from the wrong side at A and insert needle 2 single-crochet stitches away at B (fig. 20). Bring needle up at C and insert needle diagonally at D (just above B; fig. 21). Bring needle up at E and insert needle diagonally at F (just above A) to complete the flower (fig. 22). Make the next flower 1 single-crochet stitch away from previous flower. Repeat from * around as needed. Break yarn and fasten off. Weave in ends.

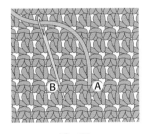

Fig. 20

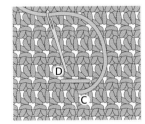

Fig. 21

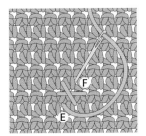

Fig. 22

This colorful, quick-to-crochet blanket makes a lovely gift for Baby. The lining adds warmth and softness and makes the blanket reversible.

Finished Size

28" x 36"

Materials

- All Seasons Cotton from Rowan (60% cotton, 40% acrylic microfiber; 50 g; 99 m) in the following amounts and colors: 🧶4🧶

A	3 skeins	185 Jazz
B	3 skeins	182 Bleached
C	3 skeins	197 Limedrop
D	1 skein	203 Giddy
E	1 skein	181 Valour
F	1 skein	205 Cheery

- Size I/9 (5.5 mm) crochet hook

- Tapestry needle

- *Optional lining:* 1¼ yards of cotton fabric at least 36" wide (be sure to preshrink); sewing needle and sewing thread

Gauge

13 sts and 11 rows = 4" in counterpane st on size I/9 hook

Counterpane Stitch

All rows: Ch 2 (do not count as st), YO, insert hook in first st, YO, draw yarn through this st and first lp on hook, YO, draw yarn through rem lps, *YO, insert hook in next st, YO, draw yarn through this st and first lp on hook, YO, draw yarn through rem lps; rep from * across.

Directions

First block: Referring to chart below, select color and ch 19. Set-up row (counts as row 1): YO, insert hook in 3rd ch from hook (do not count as st), YO, draw yarn through ch and first lp on hook, YO, draw yarn through rem lps, *YO, insert hook in next ch, YO, draw yarn through ch and first lp on hook, YO, draw through rem lps; rep from * across row—17 sts, turn. Work counterpane st for 13 more rows—1 color block complete.

Next 6 blocks: Change color and work 14 rows in counterpane st. Cont working blocks of color as indicated in chart until you have 7 blocks of color in a vertical strip.

Make 6 vertical strips.

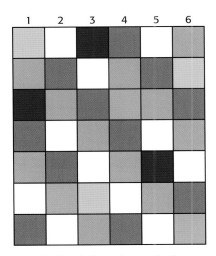

Each strip is worked vertically
in counterpane st—6 strips total.
Each square is 17 sts wide by 14 rows tall.

Finishing

Sew strips tog using overcast seam (page 19).

Edging: With RS facing (see "Joining Yarn" on page 16), work edges as follows:

With D, work 1 row counterpane st along right selvage, working 1 edge st for every row.

With A, work 1 row counterpane st along upper edge, working 1 edge st for every st.

With C, work 1 row counterpane st along left selvage, working 1 edge st for every row.

With E, work 1 row counterpane st along lower edge, working 1 edge st for every ch. Join last E st to first D st with a sl st or duplicate-st join (page 20).

Weave in ends. Block blanket according to instructions on yarn label.

Lining: Cut cotton fabric to 28" x 36" and line blanket as directed on page 21.

From the Heart

For a unique and truly special shower gift, consider getting a group of Mommy's friends together and having each of them crochet a strip of the Rainbow Baby Blanket. You and your friends will create a keepsake that the family will treasure for years.

If one of Mommy's friends doesn't crochet, invite her to participate by stitching the lining fabric to the blanket. Use a soft cotton flannel (always prewash!) for an extra-cuddly lining.

Here's a baby gift you can crochet in just a few hours. The soft yarn and vivid, pretty colors make this hat a sure winner.

Finished Sizes

0–6 mos (1 yr, 2 yrs, 3–4 yrs)

15½ (17, 18¾, 20½)"

Note: *The yarns listed below will yield a two-color hat. See "From the Heart" on page 27 if you'd like to make a multicolored hat.*

Materials

- 🤍 All Seasons Cotton from Rowan (60% cotton, 40% acrylic microfiber; 50 g; 99 m) in the following amounts and colors: 🔲

    | A | 1 skein | 181 Valour |
    | B | 1 skein | 203 Giddy |

    Sample also shown in 197 Limedrop and 185 Jazz.

- 🤍 Size J/10 (6 mm) crochet hook
- 🤍 Split-ring marker
- 🤍 Tapestry needle

Gauge

14 sts and 16 rnds = 4" in sc on J/10 hook

Two skeins of yarn is enough to make two hats, as long as you reverse the color placement.

Directions

The crown of this hat is worked in a spiral.

With A, ch 2. Work 6 sc in 2nd ch from hook, pm in first sc worked, do not turn.

Rnd 1: Work 2 sc in marked st (this will join work into a circle), 2 sc in next 5 sts—12 sts. Pm in last st of rnd, then move marker to last st of each subsequent rnd.

Rnd 2: *Sc in next st, work 2 sc in next st; rep from * around—18 sts.

Rnd 3: *Sc in next 2 sts, work 2 sc in next st; rep from * around—24 sts.

Rnd 4: *Sc in next 3 sts, work 2 sc in next st; rep from * around—30 sts.

Rnd 5: *Sc in next 4 sts, work 2 sc in next st; rep from * around—36 sts.

Rnd 6: *Sc in next 5 sts, work 2 sc in next st; rep from * around—42 sts.

Rnd 7: *Sc in next 6 sts, work 2 sc in next st; rep from * around—48 sts.

Rnd 8: *Sc in next 7 sts, work 2 sc in next st; rep from * around—54 sts. Size 0–6 mos, go to **.

Rnd 9: *Sc in next 8 sts, work 2 sc in next st; rep from * around—60 sts. Size 1 yr, go to **.

Rnd 10: *Sc in next 9 sts, work 2 sc in next st; rep from * around—66 sts. Size 2 yrs, go to **.

Rnd 11: *Sc in next 10 sts, work 2 sc in next st; rep from * around—72 sts. Size 3–4 yrs, go to **.

**All sizes: With B, sc for 12 rnds without inc.

With A, sc 1 rnd. Join last st of rnd to first st of rnd with a sl st or duplicate-st join (page 20). Break yarn and fasten off.

From the Heart

You can use your leftover yarn from the Rainbow Baby Blanket on page 22 to make a matching rainbow version of the Sweet Baby Hat in the 0–6 months size. Simply work the crown increases in white; then work 3 rows each of the remaining colors in the following order: pink, yellow, yellowish green, and aqua. Work the final row of single crochet in plum.

For a rainbow hat in a larger size, you'll need more yarn than what you'd have left over from the blanket. If you do get all-new skeins, you should be able to make a multitude of rainbow hats, as long as the crown-increase section is worked in a different color on each hat.

Simple and sweet, these booties work up fast and will keep Baby's toes warm and cozy. The ribbon helps the booties stay put while adding a colorful accent.

Finished Size

Foot circumference: 4"

Foot length: 2½"

Materials

- 1 skein of Cotton Cashmere from Debbie Bliss (85% cotton, 15% cashmere; 50 g; 95 m), color 4 Orange **3**

- Size H/8 (5 mm) crochet hook

- Split-ring marker

- Tapestry needle

- 1 yard of ⅜"-wide ribbon

Gauge

18 sts and 20 rows = 4" in sc on size H/8 hook

> **TIP**
>
> *Need a different-sized bootie? Simply follow the directions as written, using a finer yarn and smaller hook for a smaller bootie, or a bulkier yarn and larger hook for a bigger bootie.*

Foot

Ch 2. Work 6 sc in 2nd ch from hook, pm in first sc worked, do not turn.

Rnd 1: Work 2 sc in marked st (this will join work into a circle), 2 sc in next 5 sts—12 sts. Pm in last st of rnd, then move marker to last st of each subsequent rnd.

Rnd 2: *Sc in next 5 sts, work 2 sc in next st; rep from * around—14 sts.

Rnd 3: *Sc in next 6 sts, work 2 sc in next st; rep from * around—16 sts.

Rnd 4: *Sc in next 7 sts, work 2 sc in next st; rep from * around—18 sts.

Sc 5 rnds even.

Heel

Sc in first st, turn, remove marker.

(Ch 1, sc in next 14 sts, turn) 2 times.

Ch 1, sc in next 4 sts, sc2tog 3 times, sc in last 4 sts, turn—11 sts.

Ch 1, sc in next 11 sts, turn.

Ch 1, sc in next 4 sts, sc3tog, sc in last 4 sts, turn— 9 sts.

Ch 1, sc in next 9 sts. Break yarn and fasten off.

Finishing

Sew center-back heel seam. Then attach yarn at center-back heel and sc 2 rows around foot opening. Finish last rnd by joining last st of rnd to first st of rnd with a sl st or duplicate-st join (page 20). Break yarn and fasten off. Weave in ends.

Cut ribbon into two 18" lengths. Thread through tapestry needle and weave in and out of spaces between stitches around foot opening. Trim ribbon to desired length.

Options and tips for making the booties:

♥ To keep the ribbon from slipping out of the booties, tack each ribbon into place at the back of the heel with a sewing needle and thread.

♥ Grosgrain ribbon is another pretty option, and it is less slippery than satin ribbon.

♥ Because they require so little yarn, booties are a great way to use up the odds and ends of stash yarn. Just be sure to adjust your hook size to the weight of the yarn you are using.

♥ Colorful take-out containers, available at many paper, craft, and party-supply stores, are a fun a way to package the booties for gift giving.

From the Heart

Premature babies need booties to warm their tiny tootsies. Why not make several pairs to give to your local hospital's preemie ward? If you'd like to help some little one stay cozy from head to toe, see page 74 for instructions on making no-gauge preemie hats.

With a quick-to-learn pattern and no finishing other than working in ends, this reversible baby blanket looks impressive but is easy to make. I used an ultrasoft cashmere-cotton blend, luxurious but still machine washable.

Finished Size

32" x 33½"

Materials

♥ 10 skeins of Cotton Cashmere from Debbie Bliss (85% cotton, 15% cashmere; 50 g; 95 m), color 5 Orange

♥ Size H/8 (5 mm) crochet hook

♥ Tapestry needle

Gauge

18 sts and 10 rows = 4" in patt on size H/8 hook

Pattern Stitch

(Multiple of 3 + 2)

Rows 1 and 2: Ch 2 (count as st), (hdc, ch 1, hdc) in 3rd st, *sk 2 sts, (hdc, ch 1, hdc) in next st; rep from * to last 2 sts, sk 1 st, hdc in top of tch, turn.

Row 3: Ch 3 (count as st), work 3 dc in 3rd st, *sk 2 sts, work 3 dc in next st; rep from * to last 2 sts, sk 1 st, dc in top of tch, turn.

Rep rows 1–3.

Because this blanket has an odd number of rows in the patt, there is no RS or WS row.

Directions

Dbl ch 143 sts (see page 11).

> **TIP**
>
> *Remember, when working a long chain, you can always chain a few extra stitches and then pull out any unused chains.*

Set-up row: Ch 2 (count as st), (hdc, ch 1, hdc) in 5th st from hook, *sk 2 sts, (hdc, ch 1, hdc) in next ch; rep from * to last 2 ch, sk 1 ch, hdc in last ch, turn.

Beg patt, starting with row 2 (set-up row counts as row 1 first time through). Rep rows 1–3 of patt st until blanket is about 33" long, ending with completed row 3. Work rows 1 and 2 once more. Break yarn and fasten off. Weave in ends.

From the Heart

If you need the ultimate gift for your favorite mom-to-be, the Pretty Baby Blanket, the Pretty Pink Hat on page 33, and the Booties on page 28—made in matching colors—combine to create a beautiful heirloom baby set.

Elegant and deceptively easy to make, this hat looks great on babies, children, and adults. A simple pattern with a slight bias creates the coordinating all-season scarf.

Finished Sizes

Hat: 6 mos–1 yr (2–4 yrs, 5 yrs–Adult)

17 (18¾, 20½)" *This combination of yarn and stitch pattern creates a stretchy fabric. The hat fits snugly and will accommodate a range of head sizes.*

Scarf: 4" x 53"

Materials for Hat

♥ 1 skein of Cotton Cashmere from Debbie Bliss (85% cotton, 15% cashmere; 50 g; 95 m), color 7 Pink 🔳

♥ Split-ring marker

Materials for Scarf

♥ 2 skeins of Cotton Cashmere from Debbie Bliss, color 7 Pink 🔳

Materials for Hat and Scarf

♥ Size I/9 (5.5 mm) crochet hook

♥ Tapestry needle

Gauge

Hat: 14 sts and 10 rnds = 4" in crossed half double crochet on size I/9 hook

Scarf: 18 sts and 9 rows = 4" in patt on I/9 hook

Crossed Half Double Crochet Stitch

(Worked in the rnd)

All rnds: Ch 2 (count as st), *sk next st, hdc in next st, hdc in previously skipped st; rep from * around, end with hdc, join with sl st in top of beg ch.

To help you find the skipped stitch when working crossed half double crochet, put a marker in it.

Hat

Ch 3 at beg of rnd counts as a st.

Ch 5 and join into ring with sl st.

Rnd 1: Ch 3, work 11 dc in ring, sl st in top of beg ch—12 sts.

Rnd 2: Ch 3, dc in base of ch, work 2 dc in next 11 sts, sl st in top of beg ch—24 sts.

Rnd 3: Ch 3, work 2 dc in next st, (dc in next st, work 2 dc in next st) 11 times, sl st in top of tch—36 sts.

Rnd 4: Ch 3, dc in next st, work 2 dc in next st, (dc in next 2 sts, work 2 dc in next st) 11 times, sl st in top of beg ch—48 sts.

Rnd 5: Ch 3, dc in next 2 sts, work 2 dc in next st, (dc in next 3 sts, work 2 dc in next st) 11 times, sl st in top of beg ch—60 sts.

For Six Months–One Year
Go to ** below.

For Two–Four Years
Rnd 6: Ch 3, dc in next 8 sts, work 2 dc in next st, (dc in next 9 sts, work 2 dc in next st) 5 times, sl st in top of beg ch—66 sts. Go to **.

For Five Years–Adult
Rnd 6: Ch 3, dc in next 3 sts, work 2 dc in next st, (dc in next 4 sts, work 2 dc in next st) 11 times, sl st in top of beg ch—72 sts. Go to **.

**Work in crossed half double crochet for 5 (6, 9) rnds.

> **TIP**
>
> *It's easy to accidentally work into the slip stitch that joins one round to another, causing you to increase stitches where you didn't intend to. A marker in the slip stitch serves as a helpful reminder not to work into it.*

Next rnd: Ch 1, sc around, join last sc to first sc with a sl st or duplicate-st join (page 20). Break yarn and fasten off. Weave in ends.

Scarf

Ch 19, sc in 2nd ch from hook and in each ch across—18 sts; turn.

Set-up row: Ch 2 (count as st), sk first st, *sk next st, hdc in next st, hdc in skipped st; rep from * across, turn.

Row 1: Ch 3 (count as st), sk first st, *work 2 dc in next st, sk next st; rep from * across, end with dc in top of tch, turn.

Row 2: Ch 2 (count as st), sk first st, *sk next st, hdc in next st, hdc in skipped st; rep from * across, end with hdc in top of tch, turn.

Rep rows 1 and 2 until scarf is 53" long, ending with completed row 2.

Last row: Ch 1, sc in first st (base of tch), sc in next 17 sts (do not sc in tch from previous row). Break yarn and fasten off. Weave in ends.

From the Heart

Many support groups for breast cancer use a pink ribbon as a symbol to promote awareness of the disease. If you or someone you know has been affected by breast cancer, consider crocheting one of these scarves in recognition of the experience. You could also make one for everyone you know who has been affected, to wear when participating in breast-cancer awareness and fund-raising events.

Who wouldn't be cheered by these happy little puppets?

Finished Size

Approx 4" tall

Materials

♥ Small amounts of DK-weight yarn in a variety of colors. **③** The samples shown were made with Provence from Classic Elite (100% mercerized cotton; 100 g; 205 yds) in the following colors:

Flower

A	2633 Bright Yellow
B	2681 Chartreuse
C	2625 Rose Pink
D	2653 Deep Purple

Sample also shown in 2633 Bright Yellow, 2681 Chartreuse, 2695 Coral, and 2653 Deep Purple.

Chicken

A	2633 Bright Yellow
B	2695 Coral
C	2648 Nordic Blue

♥ Size H/8 (5 mm) crochet hook

♥ Split-ring marker

♥ Tapestry needle

Gauge

18 sts and 20 rnds = 4" in sc on size H/8 hook

Flower

Work through the following instructions to make the flower.

Face

With A, ch 2. Work 5 sc in 2nd ch from hook, pm in first sc worked, do not turn.

Rnd 1: Work 2 sc in marked st (this will join work into a circle), 2 sc in next 5 sts—10 sts. Pm in last st of rnd, then move marker to last st of each subsequent rnd.

Rnd 2: Work 2 sc in each st—20 sts.

Rnd 3: *Sc in next 3 sts, work 2 sc in next st; rep from * around—25 sts.

Rnds 4–8: Sc around.

Rnd 9: Sc in next 2 sts, sc2tog, *sc in next st, sc2tog; rep from * around—17 sts.

Rnd 10: Sc around. Break A, fasten off, and weave in ends.

> TIP
>
> *Because of the puppet's narrow circumference, it is best to weave in ends as you go.*

With D, make 2 eyes with French knots. With C, make a French knot for the mouth (page 21).

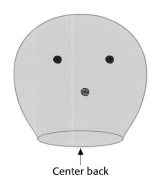

Center back

Chicken and Flower Faces

Stem

Join B at center back and sc 1 rnd.

Next rnd: Sc in next 3 sts, sc2tog, sc in next 7 sts, sc2tog, sc in next 3 sts—15 sts.

Work even in sc until stem measures 2" or desired height. Finish last rnd by joining last st of rnd to first st of rnd with sl st or duplicate-st join (page 20). Break yarn and fasten off. Weave in ends.

Petals

With C, ch 35. Work 2 dc in 4th ch from hook, ch 3, sl st in next ch, *ch 3, work 2 dc in next ch, ch 3, sl st in next ch; rep from * to end of ch—16 petals. Break yarn, leaving a long tail. Using the long tail and starting at a lower corner of flower's face, sew petals around face.

> TIP
>
> *To sew the petals around the flower face in a straight line, use pins or a length of contrast-color yarn to mark out your sewing path. Also, use knots to secure your seaming yarn, because simple weaving may not be strong enough to keep little hands from pulling off the petals.*

Leaves

With B, ch 9. Work 2 dc in 4th ch from hook, ch 3, sl st in next ch, *ch 3, work 2 dc in next ch, ch 3, sl st in next ch; rep from * to end of ch—3 leaves. Sew leaves just below petals, slightly off to one side.

Chicken

Work through the following instructions to make the chicken.

Comb

With B, ch 15. Work 2 dc in 4th ch from hook, ch 3, sl st in next ch, *ch 3, work 2 dc in next ch, ch 3, sl st in next ch; rep from * to end of ch—6 points. Break yarn and fasten off.

Head

With A, work as for flower face through rnd 10, but do not break yarn. Sew comb to head, starting at center back and centering comb so that 4 points are on back of head and 2 points are down front.

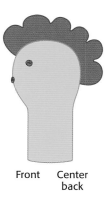

Front   Center back

With C, make eyes on either side of comb with French knots. With B, make a French knot for beak (page 21).

Body

With A, sc in next 3 sts, sc2tog, sc in next 7 sts, sc2tog, sc in next 3 sts—15 sts.

Work even in sc until body measures 2" or puppet is desired height. Finish last rnd by joining last st of rnd to first st of rnd with a sl st or duplicate-st join (page 20). Break yarn and fasten off. Weave in ends.

Wattle

With B, ch 5. Work 2 dc in 4th ch from hook, ch 3, sl st in next ch—1 point. Break yarn and fasten off. Sew wattle to center front where head and body join.

Outer Tail Feathers

With B, ch 15. Work 2 dc in 4th ch from hook, ch 3, sl st in next ch, *ch 3, work 2 dc in next ch, ch 3, sl st in next ch; rep from * to end of chain—6 feathers. Break yarn and fasten off. Sew to back of puppet as shown.

Inner Tail Feathers

With B, ch 13. Work 2 dc in 4th ch from hook, ch 3, sl st in next ch, *ch 3, work 2 dc in next ch, ch 3, sl st in next ch; rep from * to end of chain—5

feathers. Break yarn and fasten off. Sew in place as shown. Weave in ends.

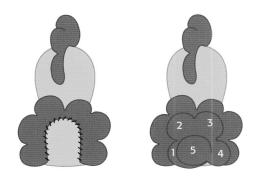

Tail Feathers

From the Heart

Once you're familiar with the components of the puppets (basic body, French knots, petals, points, and feathers), you can modify them to create your own personalized puppets. I love the idea of using them as stocking stuffers during the holiday season. Imagine waking up to find these happy faces gazing at you from the top of your stocking!

 Crochet lends itself to dimensional designs like these flowers. Use them to embellish other crochet projects or to make floral pins and hair clips.

Materials

♥ Small amounts of DK-weight yarn in a variety of colors. **3** The samples shown were made with Provence from Classic Elite (100% mercerized cotton; 100 g; 205 yds) in the following colors:

2633 Bright Yellow

2695 Coral

2625 Rose Pink

2653 Deep Purple

2648 Nordic Blue

2681 Chartreuse

♥ Size 7 (4.5 mm) crochet hook

♥ Tapestry needle

♥ *Optional:* Hair clips and/or pin backs (available at most craft, fabric, and bead stores)

Gauge

18 sts and 20 rows = 4" in sc on size 7 hook

Simple Flower 1

Ch 5, join into ring with sl st.

Ch 3, work 9 dc in ring, join last dc to top of ch with sl st—10 sts.

*Ch 2, work 2 dc in next st, ch 2, sl st in next st; rep from * around.

Break yarn and fasten off.

Simple Flower 1 (Chartreuse) and Simple Flower 2 (Coral)

Simple Flower 2

This flower has bigger petals and a more open center than Simple Flower 1.

Ch 6, join in ring with sl st.

Ch 1, work 15 sc in ring, joining last sc to first sc with sl st—15 sts.

*Ch 3, dc2tog in next st 2 times, ch 3, sl st in next st; rep from * around.

Break yarn and fasten off.

Two-Tone Flower

This two-color flower can also be made in one color.

With color 1, ch 5, join into ring with sl st.

Ch 1, work 10 sc in ring, join last st to first st with sl st.

41

Ch 1, work 10 sc around, join last sc to first sc with sl st. Break A, leaving last lp on hook.

With color 2, *ch 2, work 2 dc in next st, ch 2, sl st in next st; rep from * around.

Break yarn and fasten off.

Combo Flower

Two-Tone Flower and Solid-Color Flower

Flower Center

Ch 4. Sk first ch, sc in next 3 ch. Break yarn.

Sew short ends of fabric tog. You don't have to do this perfectly; you're just making a ball shape to fill in the hole created by the starting ring of the flower.

To make a larger center, make a longer starting ch, sk first ch, sc in rem ch.

Combo Flower

Make one Simple Flower 1 *or* Simple Flower 2, 1 Two-Tone Flower, and 1 Flower Center. Sew Two-Tone Flower on Simple Flower; tack Flower Center in center opening.

Clover Leaves

Ch 4, join into ring with sl st.

Ch 1, work 6 sc in ring, join last sc to first sc with sl st—6 sts.

*Ch 2, work 2 dc in next st, ch 2, sl st in next st; rep from * around.

Break yarn and fasten off.

Clover Leaves

42

Spiral Flowers and Leaves

To make a Spiral Flower, make a chain of any length and then work 4 dc into each chain. This will give you a narrow, spiraling piece of fabric. To form the flower, start at one end of the spiral and coil the fabric around itself, working in a free-form manner. You want the shape to be irregular and asymmetrical because this looks more interesting and natural. Once you've formed your flower, use a tapestry needle threaded with yarn to tack the spiral into place, sewing the "petals" together as needed for the flower to hold its shape and working as close to the center of the flower as possible. Complex motifs involving multiple flowers and leaves may be sewn to crinoline (available at fabric stores) before being sewn to the final garment.

To make Leaves, use green yarn and construct as for Spiral Flower but rather than coiling it around itself, arrange it behind your flower motif so that it looks like greenery.

Basic Spiral Flower

Ch 24. Work 3 dc in 4th ch from hook. Work 4 dc in each of next 20 chs. Break yarn and fasten off. Form spiral into flower shape.

Two-Tone Spiral Flower

With color 1, ch 24. Work 3 dc in 4th ch from hook, 4 dc in each of next 6 chs. Change to color 2 and work 4 dc in each rem ch. Break yarn and fasten off. Form spiral into flower shape.

For a larger flower, start with a longer chain. I started with a 48-st ch for the large spiral flowers shown here. To make the flower two-tone, work ch and first ⅓ of ch sts in color 1, and rem ⅔ of ch sts in color 2.

For small leaf accent, start with a chain of about 10 sts.

Two-Tone Spiral Flower

Spiral Flowers and Leaves

Hair Clips and Pins

Make flowers as desired and sew to pin backs or hair clips. To get the needle through the holes in the clips or pins, you may need a tapestry needle with a smaller eye than those usually sold in yarn shops. Check out your local fabric store. If you can't fit your yarn through the eye of this smaller needle, use embroidery floss instead of yarn to sew on the flowers.

FLORAL WRISTBANDS AND CHOKER

Brighten up your wardrobe with these colorful flowered bands.

Finished Sizes

Child (Adult)

Wrist Bands: 6½ (7½)" unbuttoned

Choker: 13½ (14½)" unbuttoned

You'll lose about 1" in circumference once the bands are buttoned. Length can be adjusted by starting with a few extra chains for a longer band or fewer chains for a shorter band.

Materials

♥ Small amounts of DK-weight yarn in a variety of colors. **(3)** The samples shown were made with Provence from Classic Elite (100% mercerized cotton; 100 g; 205 yds) in the following colors:

2633 Bright Yellow

2695 Coral

2625 Rose Pink

2653 Deep Purple

2648 Nordic Blue

2681 Chartreuse

♥ Size 7 (4.5 mm) crochet hook

♥ Tapestry needle

♥ ⅜"- to ½"-diameter button(s)

♥ Sewing thread

♥ Sewing needle

Gauge

18 sts and 20 rows = 4" in sc on size 7 hook

Basic Cuff

With desired color, ch 31 (35). Sc in 2nd ch from hook and in each ch across—30 (34) sts, turn.

Rows 1, 2, 4, and 5: Ch 1, sc in next 30 (34) sts, turn.

Row 3 (buttonhole row): Ch 1, sc in next 2 sts, ch 2, sk 2 sts, sc to end of row, turn.

Break yarn and fasten off.

TIP

It's perfectly legal to single crochet under the front loop only of the buttonhole chain if this is easier for you than working under the entire chain.

Block cuff so it lies flat. Sew button(s) to cuff to correspond with buttonhole(s). Make flowers as desired (see page 40 for flower instructions) and sew to cuff. Use knots to secure your sewing yarn.

Wide Cuff

With desired color, ch 31 (35). Sc in 2nd ch from hook and in each ch across—30 (34) sts, turn.

Rows 1, 2, 4, 5, and 6: Ch 1, sc in next 30 (34) sts, turn.

Row 3 (buttonhole row): Ch 1, sc in next 2 sts, ch 2, sk 2 sts, sc to end of row, turn.

Rep rows 3–6 until cuff is desired width, ending after completing row 5 on final rep.

Break yarn and fasten off. Finish as for basic cuff.

Choker

With desired color, ch 62 (66). Sc in 2nd ch from hook and in each ch across—61 (65) sts, turn.

Rows 1, 2, 4, and 5: Ch 1, sc in next 61 (65) sts, turn.

Row 3 (buttonhole row): Ch 1, sc in next 2 sts, ch 2, sk 2 sts, sc to end of row, turn.

Break yarn and fasten off. Finish as for basic cuff.

From the Heart

Here's a clever way to use these bands: button one around a gift box to create a unique package with wearable "gift wrap."

Once you understand the basic construction of the Floral Wristbands, you can explore variations to make your own unique versions. Here are some suggestions to get you started:

♥ Rather than sewing the flowers to the band, make snap-on flowers in many colors so that you can change the flowers to match your outfits.

♥ Use vintage buttons instead of flowers to decorate the bands. Sew the buttons in place or use snaps for more options.

♥ I've decorated the bands with just a few flowers, but why not make a band completely covered with blooms—a garden for your wrist!

♥ The length of the band can be adjusted to become a headband for a baby or an adult. You may want to make two or three columns of buttonholes for an adjustable fit and to allow for stretching over time.

X

This classic crochet hat is worked in a solid color or playful stripes. An optional crochet flower adds a romantic touch to this timeless style.

Finished Sizes

2 yrs (3–4 yrs, 5 yrs–Adult)

18½ (20, 21½)"

Materials

- Provence from Classic Elite (100% mercerized cotton; 100 g; 205 yds) in the following colors: 3

Solid-Color Hat
1 skein of 2625 Rose Pink

Striped Hat
Given yarn amount is enough to make 3 striped hats in any size.

A	1 skein	2648 Nordic Blue
B	1 skein	2681 Chartreuse
C	1 skein	2695 Coral

Sample also shown in 2681 Chartreuse, 2625 Rose Pink, and 2695 Coral.

- Size H/8 (5 mm) crochet hook
- Split-ring marker
- Tapestry needle
- *Optional:* Small amounts of additional colors for flower embellishment

Gauge

18 sts and 20 rnds = 4" in sc on size H/8 hook

Solid-Color Hat

Ch 2. Work 6 sc in 2nd ch from hook, pm in first sc worked, do not turn.

Rnd 1: Work 2 sc in marked st (this will join work into a circle), 2 sc in next 5 sts—12 sts. Pm in last st of rnd, then move marker to last st of each subsequent rnd.

Rnd 2: *Sc in next st, work 2 sc in next st; rep from * around—18 sts.

Rnd 3: *Sc in next 2 sts, work 2 sc in next st; rep from * around—24 sts.

Rnd 4: *Sc in next 3 sts, work 2 sc in next st; rep from * around—30 sts.

Rnd 5: *Sc in next 4 sts, work 2 sc in next st; rep from * around—36 sts.

Rnd 6: *Sc in next 5 sts, work 2 sc in next st; rep from * around—42 sts.

Rnd 7: *Sc in next 6 sts, work 2 sc in next st; rep from * around—48 sts.

Rnd 8: *Sc in next 7 sts, work 2 sc in next st; rep from * around—54 sts.

Rnd 9: *Sc in next 8 sts, work 2 sc in next st; rep from * around—60 sts.

Rnd 10: *Sc in next 9 sts, work 2 sc in next st; rep from * around—66 sts.

Rnd 11: *Sc in next 10 sts, work 2 sc in next st; rep from * around—72 sts.

Rnd 12: *Sc in next 11 sts, work 2 sc in next st; rep from * around—78 sts.

Rnd 13: *Sc in next 12 sts, work 2 sc in next st; rep from * around—84 sts. (Size 2 yrs, go to ** on page 49)

Rnd 14: *Sc in next 13 sts, work 2 sc in next st; rep from * around—90 sts. (Size 3–4 yrs, go to **).

Rnd 15: *Sc in next 14 sts, work 2 sc in next st; rep from * around—96 sts. (Size 5 yrs–Adult, go to **).

**Cont in sc without inc until hat measures 6½ (7, 7½)" from start, moving marker to last st of every rnd.

Work 1 rnd blo sc, join last st of rnd to first st of rnd with sl st or duplicate-st join (page 20). Break yarn and fasten off. Weave in ends.

Optional: Make flower or flowers of your choice and sew to hat (page 40).

Striped Hat

Starting with A, work as for solid-color hat through rnd 2.

Begin stripe patt with rnd 3, while cont shaping as for solid-color hat.

Stripe Pattern

Do not break yarns between rnds; carry them up inside of work (see "Joining Yarn" on page 16).

   2 rnds with B

   1 rnd with A

   2 rnds with C

   1 rnd with A

Rep stripe patt sequence for length of hat, ending with a completed stripe B or C (the color you end with will vary with the size you're making). Break both B and C.

With A, work 1 rnd sc. Then work 1 rnd blo sc, join last st of rnd to first st of rnd with sl st or duplicate-st join (page 20). Break yarn and fasten off. Weave in ends.

From the Heart

Crisis centers and homeless shelters can use hat donations year-round. To find out how to donate, contact the shelter directly, or ask your knitting guild or church if they have a community-service program. If they don't, consider starting one yourself!

FINGERLESS MITTS

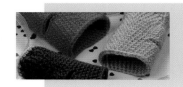

Keep your hands warm while still being able to use your fingers!

Finished Sizes

Child Small (Child Medium/Adult Small, Adult Medium, Adult Large)

Hand circumference: 5¾ (7, 8½, 10)"

Materials

♥ Topaz from Louet Sales (100% merino wool; 100 g; 175 yds) in the following amounts and colors: (4)

A   1 skein   26 Crabapple Blossom

B   small amount   55 Willow

Samples also shown in 62 Citrus Orange and 26 Crabapple Blossom; 54 Teal and 55 Willow.

♥ Size 7 (4.5 mm) crochet hook

♥ Size H/8 (5 mm) crochet hook

♥ Split-ring marker

♥ Tapestry needle

Gauge

17 sts and 20 rnds = 4" in sc on larger hook

Cuff

With smaller hook and A, ch 5 (6, 7, 7). Sc in 2nd ch from hook and in each ch across, turn—4 (5, 6, 6) sts.

*Ch 1, sc in first st, flo sc in next 2 (3, 4, 4) sts, sc in last st, turn.

Rep from * until you've worked 20 (26, 30, 36) rows total.

Break yarn and fasten off. Seam short edges of cuff tog.

Hand

Change to larger hook and starting at cuff seam, sc 20 (26, 30, 36) sts around top of cuff with A. Pm in last st of rnd. Sc 1 rnd.

Next rnd: Sc to last st, work 2 sc in last st—21 (27, 31, 37) sts.

Next rnd: Work 2 sc in first st, sc around—22 (28, 32, 38) sts.

Rep last 2 rnds 1 (1, 2, 2) more times—24 (30, 36, 42) sts.

Sc 3 (5, 5, 6) rnds even.

Thumb Opening

Next rnd: Ch 7 (8, 10, 11), sk next 5 (6, 7, 8) sts and sc in 6th (7th, 8th, 9th) st, sc to end of rnd.

Next rnd: Sc across 7 (8, 10, 11) chs, sc to end of rnd.

Next rnd: (Sc2tog, 2 sc) 2 (2, 3, 3) times, sc to end of rnd—24 (30, 36, 42) sts.

Work even for 4 (6, 8, 10) more rnds. Break yarn and fasten off. Weave in ends.

Finishing

With A, work 1 rnd sc along lower edge of cuff; then with B, work 1 rnd sc. Finish last rnd by joining last st of rnd to first st of rnd with sl st or duplicate-st join (page 20). Break yarn and fasten off. Weave in ends.

FOOTIES

Somewhere between a sock and a slipper,
these foot warmers are super cozy and much
faster to make than a regular sock.

Finished Sizes

2–4 yrs (4–6 yrs, Child Large/Adult Small, Adult Medium, Adult Large, Adult Extra Large)

Foot circumference: 5½ (6½, 7½, 8½, 9½, 10¼)"

Foot length: 6 (7, 8, 9, 10, 11)"

Note: *These slipper socks can be worn a bit smaller or a bit larger than your actual foot size. Made small, they will stretch to accommodate your feet and fit like socks; made large, they fit like slippers.*

Materials

♥ Topaz from Louet Sales (100% merino wool; 100 g; 175 yds) in the following amounts and colors: [4]

A   1 (1, 1, 2,   26 Crabapple Blossom
     2, 2) skeins

B   small amount   55 Willow

Samples also shown in 62 Citrus Orange and 26 Crabapple Blossom; 54 Teal and 55 Willow.

♥ Size H/8 (5 mm) crochet hook

♥ Split-ring markers (having 2 different colors is helpful)

♥ Tapestry needle

♥ *Optional:* Fabric paint or no-slip spray (available at home-improvement and hardware stores) to give the soles some grip

Gauge

17 sts and 20 rnds = 4" in sc on H/8 hook

Right Foot

All sizes: With A, ch 8. Sc in front lp of 2nd ch from hook and in next 6 chs, do not turn, sc in next 7 chs along lower edge of ch—14 sc. Pm in last st of rnd. Move marker to last st of each subsequent rnd.

Toe Shaping

Rnd 1: Work 3 sc in next st, sc in next 6 sts, work 3 sc in next st, sc in next 6 sts—18 sts.

Rnd 2: Sc in next st, work 3 sc in next st, sc in next 8 sts, work 3 sc in next st, sc in next 7 sts—22 sts.

Rnd 3: Sc in next 2 sts, work 3 sc in next st, sc to end of rnd—24 sts. (Size 2–4 yrs, go to ** on page 54.)

Rnd 4: Sc in next 3 sts, work 3 sc in next st, sc to end of rnd—26 sts.

Rnd 5: Sc in next 4 sts, work 3 sc in next st, sc to end of rnd—28 sts. (Size 4–6 yrs, go to ** on page 54.)

Rnd 6: Sc in next 5 sts, work 3 sc in next st, sc to end of rnd—30 sts.

Rnd 7: Sc in next 6 sts, work 3 sc in next st, sc to end of rnd—32 sts. (Size Child Large/Adult Small, go to ** on page 54.)

Rnd 8: Sc in next 7 sts, work 3 sc in next st, sc to end of rnd—34 sts.

Rnd 9: Sc in next 8 sts, work 3 sc in next st, sc to end of rnd—36 sts. (Size Adult Medium, go to ** on page 54.)

Rnd 10: Sc in next 9 sts, work 3 sc in next st, sc to end of rnd—38 sts.

Rnd 11: Sc in next 10 sts, work 3 sc in next st, sc to end of rnd—40 sts. (Size Adult Large, go to **.)

Rnd 12: Sc in next 11 sts, work 3 sc in next st, sc to end of rnd—42 sts.

Rnd 13: Sc in next 12 sts, work 3 sc in next st, sc to end of rnd—44 sts. (Size Adult Extra Large, go to **.)

**Work even in sc on 24 (28, 32, 36, 40, 44) sts for 18 (20, 22, 24, 26, 28) rnds.

> **TIP**
>
> *To keep track of increases, place the marker in the center stitch of 3 single crochets worked into 1 stitch. On the next round, the increase occurs in the stitch with the marker.*

Reposition markers for foot opening: Hold slipper so that top is facing you (as if you were about to put it on). Find center-front st and mark it. It helps to put slipper on foot to confirm that marked st is at center front. Pm in 2nd (2nd, 3rd, 3rd, 4th, 4th) st to left of marked center st. This is marker A. Pm in 3rd (3rd, 4th, 4th, 5th, 5th) st to right of marked center st. This is marker B. If you have different-colored markers, use different colors for A and B so you can tell them apart. You should have 6 (6, 8, 8, 10, 10) sts marked off, centered around center-front st marker. Remove markers at center-front foot and beg of rnd; markers A and B remain.

Heel

Sc around slipper, stopping at marker A (do not work into marked st), turn.

Ch 1, sc across next 18 (22, 24, 28, 30, 34) heel sts, stopping at marker B (do not work into marked st), turn.

(Ch 1, sc across heel sts, turn) for 6 (8, 8, 10, 10, 12) rows. Break yarn. Remove markers.

Heel Flap

With RS of heel sts facing you, rejoin yarn in 6th (8th, 8th, 10th, 10th, 12th) st from end (page 16) and sc across center 6 (6, 8, 8, 10, 10) heel-flap sts, turn.

(Ch 1, sc across heel-flap sts, turn) for 6 (8, 8, 10, 10, 12) rows. Break yarn.

Finishing

Sew heel-flap seams with overcast st from RS (page 19).

Sew heel-flap seams.

Trim: Rejoin yarn at center-back heel. With A, sc 2 rnds around foot opening; then with B, sc 1 rnd B. Finish last rnd by joining last st of rnd to first st of rnd with sl st or duplicate-st join (page 20). Break yarn and fasten off.

Weave in ends. Block footie into shape.

> **TIP**
>
> *Because it is worked in a long, narrow spiral, the footie will have a slight torque or twist, which will disappear as soon as the footie is put on and actually helps it hug your foot more closely.*

Left Foot

Work left foot as for right, reversing toe shaping as follows.

Left Toe Shaping

Rnd 1: Work 3 sc in next st, sc in next 6 sts, work 3 sc in next st, sc in next 6 sts—18 sts.

Rnd 2: Sc in next st, work 3 sc in next st, sc in next 8 sts, work 3 sc in next st, sc in next 7 sts—22 sts.

Rnd 3: Sc in next 13 sts, work 3 sc in next st, sc to end of rnd—24 sts. (Size 2–4 yrs, go to ** on page 54.)

Rnd 4: Sc in next 14 sts, work 3 sc in next st, sc to end of rnd—26 sts.

Rnd 5: Sc in next 15 sts, work 3 sc in next st, sc to end of rnd—28 sts. (Size 4–6 yrs, go to ** on page 54.)

Rnd 6: Sc in next 16 sts, work 3 sc in next st, sc to end of rnd—30 sts.

Rnd 7: Sc in next 17 sts, work 3 sc in next st, sc to end of rnd—32 sts. (Size Child Large/Adult Small, go to ** on page 54.)

Rnd 8: Sc in next 18 sts, work 3 sc in next st, sc to end of rnd—34 sts.

Rnd 9: Sc in next 19 sts, work 3 sc in next st, sc to end of rnd—36 sts. (Size Adult Medium, go to ** on page 54.)

Rnd 10: Sc in next 20 sts, work 3 sc in next st, sc to end of rnd—38 sts.

Rnd 11: Sc in next 21 sts, work 3 sc in next st, sc to end of rnd—40 sts. (Size Adult Large, go to ** on page 54.)

Rnd 12: Sc in next 22 sts, work 3 sc in next st, sc to end of rnd—42 sts.

Rnd 13: Sc in next 23 sts, work 3 sc in next st, sc to end of rnd—44 sts. (Size Adult Extra Large, go to ** on page 54.)

Work rem of left foot as for right foot.

From the Heart

A coordinating set of Fingerless Mitts (see page 50) and Footies makes a great birthday or holiday gift. Since they work up quickly, you can make a set for each member of the family.

 *My kitty **loves** her felted bed!*

Finished Size

17" to 18" diameter, felted

Materials

♥ 1 skein of Lamb's Pride Worsted from Brown Sheep Company (85% wool, 15% mohair; 4 oz; 190 yds) in each of the following colors: (**4**)

    A   M-190 Jaded Dreams

    B   M-78 Aztec Turquoise

    C   M-120 Limeade

    Sample also shown in M-80 Blue Blood Red, M-38 Lotus Pink, and M-22 Autumn Harvest.

♥ Size K/10.5 (6.5 mm) crochet hook

♥ Split-ring marker

♥ Tapestry needle

Gauge

12 sts and 7 rows = 4" in dc on size K/10.5 hook

Directions

Ch 3 at beg of rnds counts as a st.

With A, ch 6 and join into ring with sl st.

Rnd 1: Ch 3, work 10 dc in ring, sl st in top of beg ch—11 sts.

Rnd 2: Ch 3, dc in base of ch, work 2 dc in next 10 sts, sl st in top of beg ch—22 sts.

Rnd 3: Ch 3, work 2 dc in next st, (dc in next st, work 2 dc in next st) 10 times, sl st in top of beg ch—33 sts.

Rnd 4: Ch 3, dc in next st, work 2 dc in next st, (dc in next 2 sts, work 2 dc in next st) 10 times, sl st in top of beg ch—44 sts.

Rnd 5: Ch 3, dc in next 2 sts, work 2 dc in next st, (dc in next 3 sts, work 2 dc in next st) 10 times, sl st in top of beg ch—55 sts.

Rnd 6: Ch 3, dc in next 3 sts, work 2 dc in next st, (dc in next 4 sts, work 2 dc in next st) 10 times, sl st in top of beg ch—66 sts.

Cont in this manner, inc 11 sts every rnd and working 1 more dc before each inc with each subsequent rnd until you complete rnd 11.

Rnd 12: Ch 3, dc in next 9 sts, work 2 dc in next st, (dc in next 10 sts, work 2 dc in next st) 10 times, sl st in top of beg ch, changing to B with final sl st.—132 sts. Break A.

With B, cont as established, inc 11 sts every rnd and working 1 more dc before each inc with each subsequent rnd until you complete 5 rnds of B.

Rnd 6: Ch 3, dc in next 15 sts, work 2 dc in next st, (dc in next 16 sts, work 2 dc in next st) 10 times, sl st in top of beg ch, changing to C with final sl st—198 sts. Break B.

Border

Use C throughout.

Rnd 1: Ch 3, work flo dc around without working any increases, sl st in top of ch at end of rnd.

Rnds 2 and 3: Ch 3, dc around, sl st in top of ch at end of rnd.

Rep rnds 1–3 once more; this forms inner facing of sides. Break yarn. Fold facing in toward center of bed along fold line made on 2nd rep of rnd 1. Sew facing into place. Break yarn. Weave in ends.

Felting

Machine wash bed in hot water, using mild soap.

Throw in some jeans or towels to provide extra agitation, making sure not to overload machine. Remove bed before spin cycle; otherwise, you may put permanent creases into it. Repeat this one or two more times, shaping bed between washings; then throw it in the dryer and let it go for a complete cycle. Bed should now be thoroughly felted and can be machine washed and dried without any fuss. It may be a bit bigger or smaller than size given, but kitty will like it no matter what size it is!

From the Heart

Felted mats like these are ideal for animal shelters, since the felted fabric won't tear or snag and can be easily washed. You could also donate mats to raffles or silent auctions to help raise money for your favorite animal causes.

Kitty's Bed is a great project for learning how to crochet in rounds, because the felting will mask most irregularities. If you don't have a kitty in your life, this project has other uses. It can be placed under the tray beneath a potted houseplant, in the center of a table, or used as a small accent rug (you may want to apply a nonskid backing).

Another fun idea would be to make a rainbow-colored mat and use it as a tool for helping toddlers learn their colors. Or make a mat with color changes in every round—a great way to use up stash yarn.

To make a larger mat, keep increasing as established until the mat is the size you want (the mat will shrink about 30%–35%, depending on the yarn, your washing machine, and your crochet tension).

RUFFLE-EDGE HAT

Ruffles and easy embroidered accents add charm to this feminine design.

Finished Sizes

6 mos–1 yr (2–4 yrs, 5 yrs–Adult)

16¾ (19¼, 21½)"

Materials

♥ Wool Cotton from Rowan (50% wool, 50% cotton; 50 g; 123 m) in the following amounts and colors: 3

A	1 (2, 2) skeins	957 Lavish
B	1 (1, 1) skein	910 Gypsy
C	small amount	901 Citron (for embroidery)

Samples also shown in 946 Elf, 901 Citron, and 949 Aqua; 949 Aqua, 946 Elf, and 910 Gypsy.

♥ Size H/8 (5 mm) crochet hook

♥ Split-ring marker

♥ Tapestry needle

Gauge

20 sts and 22 rnds = 4" in sc with H/8 hook

Crown

With A, ch 5, join into a ring with sl st.

Rnd 1: Work 6 sc in ring. Pm in last sc of rnd. Move marker to last sc with each subsequent rnd.

Rnd 2: Work 2 sc in next 6 sts—12 sts.

Rnd 3: *Sc in next st, work 2 sc in next st; rep from * around—18 sts.

Rnd 4: *Sc in next 2 sts, work 2 sc in next st; rep from * around—24 sts.

Rnd 5: *Sc in next 3 sts, work 2 sc in next st; rep from * around—30 sts.

Rnd 6: *Sc in next 4 sts, work 2 sc in next st; rep from * around—36 sts.

Rnd 7: *Sc in next 5 sts, work 2 sc in next st; rep from * around—42 sts.

Rnd 8: *Sc in next 6 sts, work 2 sc in next st; rep from * around—48 sts.

Rnd 9: *Sc in next 7 sts, work 2 sc in next st; rep from * around—54 sts.

Rnd 10: *Sc in next 8 sts, work 2 sc in next st; rep from * around—60 sts.

Cont in this manner, inc 6 sts per rnd, until you complete rnd 14 (16, 18). *Sc in next 12 (14, 16) sts, work 2 sc in next st; rep from * around—84 (96, 108) sts.

Work even in sc until hat measures 5 (5¾, 6½)" from start.

Change to B and sc for 3 (3, 5) rnds. Break B.

Brim

With A, sc 1 rnd.

For Six Months–One Year (Two–Four Years)

Rnd 1: *Sc in next 6 (7) sts, work 2 sc in next st; rep from * around—96 (108) sts.

Rnd 2: *Sc in next 7 (8) sts, work 2 sc in next st; rep from * around—108 (120) sts.

Rnd 3: Sc in next 4 (4) sts, work 2 sc in next st, *sc in next 8 (9) sts, work 2 sc in next st; rep from * around, end with sc in last 4 (5) sts—120 (132) sts.

Rnd 4: Sc in next 5 (5) sts, work 2 sc in next st, *sc in next 9 (10) sts, work 2 sc in next st; rep from * around, end with sc in last 4 (5) sts—132 (144) sts.

Sc 2 (2) rnds even. Finish last rnd by joining last st of rnd to first st of rnd with sl st or duplicate-st join (page 20). Break yarn and fasten off. Weave in ends.

For Five Years–Adult

Rnd 1: *Sc in next 8 sts, work 2 sc in next st; rep from * around—120 sts.

Rnd 2: *Sc in next 9 sts, work 2 sc in next st; rep from * around—132 sts.

Rnd 3: *Sc in next 10 sts, work 2 sc in next st; rep from * around—144 sts.

Rnd 4: Sc in next 5 sts, work 2 sc in next st, *sc in next 11 sts, work 2 sc in next st; rep from * around, end with sc in last 6 sts—156 sts.

Rnd 5: Sc in next 6 sts, work 2 sc in next st, *sc in next 12 sts, work 2 sc in next st; rep from * around, end with sc in last 6 sts—168 sts.

Rnd 6: Sc in next 7 sts, work 2 sc in next st, *sc in next 13 sts, work 2 sc in next st; rep from * around, end with sc in last 6 sts—180 sts.

Sc 3 rnds even. Finish last rnd by joining last st of rnd to first st of rnd with sl st or duplicate-st join (page 20). Break yarn and fasten off. Weave in ends.

Finishing

With C, embroider flowers along band just above brim (see "Making Embroidered Flowers" on page 21).

*Proving that crochet can be lightweight and soft—
and with options for a subtle tonal palette or
a flamboyant multicolored design—this scarf
should please anyone on your gift list.*

Finished Sizes

Child/Adult Short, Three Colors: 4" x 47"

Adult Medium, Six Colors: 4" x 56¼"

Adult Long, Three Colors: 4" x 75"

Materials

♥ Wool Cotton from Rowan (50% wool, 50% cotton; 50 g; 123 m) in the following amounts and colors: (3)

Child/Adult Short: Three Colors

A	1 skein	957 Lavish
B	1 skein	901 Citron
C	1 skein	910 Gypsy

Adult Medium: Six Colors

The following quantity will make two 6-color scarves—one for you and one for a friend!

A	1 skein	901 Citron
B	1 skein	946 Elf
C	1 skein	949 Aqua
D	1 skein	957 Lavish
E	1 skein	910 Gypsy
F	1 skein	947 Spark

Adult Long: Three Colors

A	2 skeins	946 Elf
B	1 skein	949 Aqua
C	2 skeins	901 Citron

All Sizes

♥ Size H/8 (5 mm) crochet hook

♥ Tapestry needle

Gauge

23 sts and 11 rows = 4" in front loop counterpane st on H/8 hook

Front Loop Counterpane Stitch

All rows: Ch 2 (count as st), YO, insert hook in front lp of second st, YO, draw lp through this st and first lp on hook, YO, draw through rem lps, *YO, insert hook in front lp of next st, YO, draw lp through this st and first lp on hook, YO, draw through rem lps; rep from * across row, working last st in top of tch from previous row, turn.

Three-Color Scarf

Child/Adult Short (Adult Long)

With A, ch 25.

Set-up row (counts as row 1): YO, insert hook in third ch from hook, YO, draw lp through this ch and first lp on hook, YO, draw through rem lps, *YO, insert hook in next ch, YO, draw lp through this ch and first lp on hook, YO, draw through rem lps; rep from * across row—23 sts. Turn.

Work front loop counterpane st for 11 more rows with A (first block made). Then, cont patt st throughout in color sequence as follows:

1 row with B

12 rows with C

1 row with B

12 rows with A

Rep color sequence until you've completed 10 (16) total blocks. Fasten off and weave in ends.

Six-Color Scarf

Work as given for Child/Adult Short (Adult Long) scarf, placing colors as follows:

12 rows with A (set-up row followed by 11 rows of front loop counterpane st)

1 row with F

12 rows with B

1 row with A

12 rows with C

1 row with B

12 rows with D

1 row with C

12 rows with E

1 row with D

12 rows with F

1 row with E

12 rows with A

1 row with F

12 rows with B

1 row with A

12 rows with C

1 row with B

12 rows with D

1 row with C

12 rows with E

1 row with D

12 rows with F

Break yarn and fasten off. Weave in ends.

From the Heart

The Ruffle-Edge Hat (page 59) and Color-Block Scarf in coordinating colors make a lovely birthday, holiday, or back-to-school gift for the young ladies in your life.

Keep your loved ones warm with this lap-sized blanket, the perfect size for snuggling on the sofa or sitting in a favorite reading chair.

Materials

♥ 2 skeins of Topaz from Louet Sales (100% merino wool; 100 g; 175 yds) in each of the following colors: (4)

A	26 Crabapple Blossom
B	58 Burgundy
C	70 Pure White
D	42 Eggplant

♥ Size I/9 (5.5 mm) crochet hook

♥ Size K/10.5 (6.5 mm) crochet hook

♥ Tapestry needle

Gauge

8 sts and 20 rows = 4" in alternate st on size K/10.5 (6.5 mm) hook

8 sts and 14 rows = 4" in grit st on size I/9 (5.5 mm) hook

Alternate Stitch

(Worked with size K/10.5 hook)

All rows: Ch 2 (do not count as st), sk first st, work 2 sc in next st, *sk next st, work 2 sc in next st; rep from * across row.

Grit Stitch

(Worked with size I/9 hook)

All rows: Ch 1, dc in first st, *sk next st, (sc, dc) in next st; rep from * across row until 1 st remains, sc in last st.

Directions

With size I/9 hook and A, dbl ch (see page 11) 132 sts.

Rows 1 and 2: Work grit st with A.

Row 3: Cont in grit st, alternating colors as follows: cont with A, ch 1, dc in first st, *work 2 grit sts with A, 1 grit st with B; rep from * across row, ending with 2 grit sts in A, sc in last st (see "Joining Yarn in the Middle of a Row" on page 16).

Row 4: Work grit st with A.

Rows 5–8: Work alternate st with K/10.5 hook and C.

Row 9: Work alternate st with D.

Rows 10–12: Work grit st with I/9 hook and B.

For remainder of blanket, remember to always use size K/10.5 hook when working alternate stitch, and size I/9 hook when working grit stitch.

Row 13: Cont in grit st, alternating colors as follows: cont with B, ch 1, dc in first st, *work 2 grit sts with B, 1 grit st with C; rep from * across row, ending with 2 grit sts in B, sc in last st.

Rows 14–18: Work grit st with B.

Row 19: Cont in grit st, alternating colors as follows: cont with B, ch 1, dc in first st, *work 2 grit sts with B, 1 grit st with D; rep from * across row, ending with 2 grit sts in B, sc in last st.

Rows 20–22: Work grit st with B.

Rows 23–26: Work alternate st with A.

Rows 27–34: Work grit st with D.

Row 35: Cont in grit st, alternating colors as follows: cont with D, ch 1, dc in first st, *work 2 grit sts with D, 1 grit st with C; rep from * across row, ending with 2 grit sts in D, sc in last st.

Rows 36–40: Work grit st with D.

Rows 41–44: Work alternate st with C.

Row 45: Work alternate st with B.

Rows 46–48: Work grit st with A.

Rows 49–56: Work alternate st with C.

Row 57: Work alternate st with D.

Rows 58–60: Work grit st with A.

Row 61: Cont in grit st, alternating colors as follows: cont with A, ch 1, dc in first st, *work 2 grit sts with A, 1 grit st with B; rep from * across row, ending with 2 grit sts in A, sc in last st.

Row 62: Work grit st with A.

Rows 63–66: Work alternate st with B.

Row 67: Work alternate st with D.

Row 68: Work grit st with C.

Row 69: Cont in grit st, alternating colors as follows: cont with C, ch 1, dc in first st, *work 2 grit sts with C, 1 grit st with B; rep from * across row, ending with 2 grit sts in C, sc in last st.

Rows 70–72: Work grit st with C.

Rows 73–76: Work alternate st with D.

Rows 77–80: Work grit st with B.

Row 81: Cont in grit st, alternating colors as follows: cont with B, ch 1, dc in first st, *work 2 grit sts with B, 1 grit st with A; rep from * across row, ending with 2 grit sts in B, sc in last st.

Rows 82–84: Work grit st with B.

Rows 85–90: Work alternate st with D.

Row 91: Work alternate st with C.

Rows 92–94: Work grit st with A.

Row 95: Cont in grit st, alternating colors as follows: cont with A, ch 1, dc in first st, *work 2 grit sts with A, 1 grit st with C; rep from * across row, ending with 2 grit sts in A, sc in last st.

Rows 96–98: Work grit st with A.

Rows 99–102: Work alternate st with D.

Row 103: Work alternate st with B.

Rows 104–108: Work grit st with C.

Row 109: Cont in grit st, alternating colors as follows; cont with C, ch 1, dc in first st, *work 2 grit sts with C, 1 grit st with D; rep from * across row, ending with 2 grit sts in C, sc in last st.

Row 110: Work grit st with C.

Rows 111–114: Work alternate st with B.

Rows 115–116: Work grit st with A.

Rows 117–122: Work alternate st with C.

Row 123: Work alternate st with D.

Row 124: Work grit st with B.

Row 125: Work alternate st with A.

Break yarn and fasten off. Weave in ends. Block.

From the Heart

Lap-sized blankets like this one are ideal for people living in assisted-living and elder-care facilities, or for anyone who is confined to a wheelchair or has limited mobility. The smaller size makes it manageable, while the stitch pattern makes a dense, warm fabric.

Built one block at a time, this colorful scarf can be modified to any length you like by simply adding or subtracting blocks.

Finished Size

4½" x 54"

Materials

♥ Bazic Wool from Classic Elite (100% Superwash wool; 50 g; 65 yds), 1 skein in each of the following colors:

A   2932 Plum

B   2961 Pink

C   2935 Orange

D   2916 White

♥ Size K/10.5 (6.5 mm) crochet hook

♥ Tapestry needle

Note: *Since the squares need to be blocked into shape, the pattern works best in wool.*

Gauge

12 sts and 10 rows = 4" in hdc on size K/10.5 hook

Basic Block

Finished block is approx 4½" x 4½" after blocking.

Ch 2 at beg of rows does not count as a st.

Ch 3. Work 3 hdc in 3rd ch from hook, turn.

Row 1: Ch 2, hdc in first st, work 3 hdc in next st, hdc in last st, turn—5 sts.

Row 2: Ch 2, hdc in next 2 sts, work 3 hdc in next st, hdc in next 2 sts, turn—7 sts.

Row 3: Ch 2, hdc in next 3 sts, work 3 hdc in next st, hdc in next 3 sts, turn—9 sts.

Row 4: Ch 2, hdc in next 4 sts, work 3 hdc in next st, hdc in next 4 sts, turn—11 sts.

Row 5: Ch 2, hdc in next 5 sts, work 3 hdc in next st, hdc in next 5 sts, turn—13 sts.

Row 6: Ch 2, hdc in next 6 sts, work 3 hdc in next st, hdc in next 6 sts, turn—15 sts.

Row 7: Ch 2, hdc in next 7 sts, work 3 hdc in next st, hdc in next 7 sts, turn—17 sts.

Row 8: Ch 2, hdc in next 8 sts, work 3 hdc in next st, hdc in next 8 sts, turn—19 sts.

Row 9: Ch 2, hdc in next 9 sts, work 3 hdc in next st, hdc in next 9 sts, do not turn—21 sts.

TIP

Using the simple start (page 8) keeps the starting corner of the block tidy.

Edging: Ch 1, work 9 hdc evenly along side selvage, ch 1, work 1 hdc in corner (where first 3 hdc of block were worked), ch 1, work 9 hdc along 2nd selvage, ch 1, join to top edge with sl st or duplicate-st join (page 20).

Break yarn, fasten off. Block piece into a flat square. Weave in ends.

Make 12 blocks in the following (or your own) color combinations. Work edging for each block in last color used (row 9).

Block 1

Rows 1–3: White

Rows 4–6: Plum

Rows 7–9: Pink

Block 2

Rows 1–3: Plum
Rows 4–6: Pink
Rows 7–9: Orange

Block 3

Rows 1–3: Orange
Rows 4–6: Plum
Rows 7–9: Pink

Block 4

Rows 1–3: Orange
Rows 4–6: Pink
Rows 7–9: Plum

Block 5

Rows 1–9: Orange

Block 6

Rows 1–3: Pink
Rows 4–6: Orange
Rows 7–9: Plum

Block 7

Rows 1–3: Plum
Rows 4–6: White
Rows 7–9: Orange

Block 8

Rows 1–9: Pink

Block 9

Rows 1–3: Pink
Rows 4–6: Orange
Rows 7–9: White

Block 10

Rows 1–3: Plum
Rows 4–6: Orange
Rows 7–9: Pink

Block 11

Rows 1–9: Plum

Block 12

Rows 1–3: Pink
Rows 4–6: Plum
Rows 7–9: Orange

TIP

Pin a numbered slip of paper to each block, since you will be sewing them in numerical order when they are completed.

Finishing

Sew blocks tog with an overcast seam (page 19), working into 10 sts from each block. Keep them in numerical order and rotate them in different directions—this makes the design more interesting.

Edging: With white, and starting at lower corner of scarf, work blo sc around scarf edges, working 10 to 11 sc along each square and working 1 ch on either side of corner sts of scarf (not individual squares). Finish by joining last edge st to first edge st with sl st or duplicate-st join (page 20).

Break yarn and fasten off. Weave in ends. Even though individual squares have already been blocked, block scarf again now that squares are joined.

The large bag is the perfect size for carrying a notebook or magazine. The small bag features an appliquéd flower and is sized for carrying a wallet and some lipstick.

Finished Sizes

Large Bag: 9" x 12"

Small Bag: 6" x 6"

Materials

♥ Bazic Wool from Classic Elite (100% Superwash wool; 50 g; 65 yds) in the following amounts and colors: (4)

Large Bag

A	2 skeins	2932 Plum
B	1 skein	2961 Pink
C	1 skein	2935 Orange
D	1 skein	2916 White

Small Bag

A	2 skeins	2961 Pink
B	1 skein	2932 Plum
C	1 skein	2916 White

♥ Size I/9 (5.5 mm) crochet hook

♥ Tapestry needle

♥ *Optional:* Snap; sewing needle and thread

Gauge

17 sts and 17 rows = 4" in sc on size I/9 hook

Large Bag

Work through the following instructions to make the large bag.

Back

With A, ch 3. Work 3 sc in 2nd ch from hook, turn.

Row 1: Ch 1, sc in first st, work 3 sc in next st, sc in last st—5 sts. Turn.

Row 2: Ch 1, sc in next 2 sts, work 3 sc in next st, sc in next 2 sts—7 sts. Turn.

Row 3: Ch 1, sc in next 3 sts, work 3 sc in next st, sc in next 3 sts—9 sts. Turn.

Row 4: Ch 1, sc in next 4 sts, work 3 sc in next st, sc in next 4 sts—11 sts. Turn.

Cont in this manner, working 1 more sc before and after center inc st with each subsequent row until you've completed row 35.

Row 36: Ch 1, sc in next 36 sts, work 3 sc in next st, sc in next 36 sts—75 sts. Turn.

Row 37: Ch 1, sc in next 38 sts, turn.

Rep last row 11 more times. On 12th row, do not turn at end of row and do not break yarn.

Edging: With A, sc down left selvage, along bottom, up right selvage, and across top, working 1 sc per st/row and working ch 1 at each corner. Join last sc to first sc with sl st or duplicate-st join (page 20). Break yarn and fasten off.

Front

With B, work as for back, working rows 1–12 with B, 13–24 with C, and 25–36 with D (see page 17 for changing colors.) Work 12 sc rows as for back, working rows 1–4 with B, 5–8 with C, and 9–12 with D. With A, work edging as for back.

Finishing

Block front and back pieces flat. With WS tog and A, sew pieces tog with an overcast seam (page 19). With sewing needle and thread, sew snap in place on inside of bag if desired.

Strap: With A, dbl ch (page 11) to desired strap length plus 2". Keep in mind that strap will stretch when bag is carried, so measure both unstretched and stretched lengths. Straps on bags shown measure 32", unstretched. Ch 1, sc 1 row along dbl ch. Break yarn and fasten off. Block strap (it will be a bit curly when finished). Sew into place about 1" down along inside of bag.

Small Bag

Work through the following instructions to make the small bag.

Back

With A, work as for large bag through row 24— 51 sts.

Work edging as for large bag.

Front

Work as for large bag through row 24—51 sts. Break C.

With A, work edging as for large bag.

Finishing

Work as for large bag.

If desired, appliqué a flower to front of bag (page 40). I used Simple Flower 2 with a contrasting-color Flower Center.

From the Heart

Combined with the Retro Scarf (page 68), these bags make great back-to-school gifts. Or consider donating a set to your local youth shelter.

Preemies are born in a range of sizes, but they are always very small, and they need a little help keeping warm. A great way to use up leftover yarn is to make preemie hats, which can be donated to your local hospital.

Finished Size

Head Circumference: From 4¾" to 14"

Materials

- Small amount of soft, machine-washable yarn of any sock (**1**), sport (**2**), DK (**3**), or worsted (**4**) weight
- Crochet hook appropriate to yarn weight
- Split-ring marker
- Tapestry needle

Gauge

This recipe allows you to make a single-crochet preemie hat using any yarn and hook you wish, without having to worry about gauge.

Directions

With yarn and appropriate-size hook, ch 2. Work 6 sc in 2nd ch from hook, pm in first sc worked, do not turn.

Rnd 1: Work 2 sc in marked st (this will join work into a circle), 2 sc in next 5 sts—12 sts. Pm in last st of rnd, then move marker to last st of each subsequent rnd.

Rnd 2: *Sc in next st, work 2 sc in next st; rep from * around—18 sts.

Rnd 3: *Sc in next 2 sts, work 2 sc in next st; rep from * around—24 sts.

Rnd 4: *Sc in next 3 sts, work 2 sc in next st; rep from * around—30 sts.

Cont in this manner, working 1 more sc before inc st with each subsequent row until hat measures diameter for desired circumference; see table below.

Diameter	Approximate Circumference
1½"	4¾"
1¾"	5½"
2"	6¼"
2¼"	7"
2½"	7¾"
2¾"	8½"
3"	9½"
3¼"	10¼"
3½"	11"
3¾"	11¾"
4"	12½"
4¼"	13¼"
4½"	14"

Count number of inc rnds worked to this point. Now work same number of rnds without inc. For example, if you worked 6 inc rnds, you will work 6 rnds even. This will give you a hat that ends approx just above ears. To make a hat that covers ears, work even number of rnds equal to 1½ times the number of inc rnds. On a hat with 6 inc rnds, you will work 9 rnds even for a hat that covers ears.

Note: *You may need to adjust the number of rounds you work even to accommodate a pattern, such as on the striped hat shown. Not to worry—the hat will still fit some little sweetie!*

TIPS

♥ *If you want to make a hat in a circumference that isn't listed in the chart on page 75, divide the desired circumference by 3.1416 to obtain the diameter you need. For example, if you need to make a hat with a 5" circumference: 5" ÷ 3.1416 = 1.59". Although 1.59" is a little difficult to measure, you know that the diameter needs to be a bit larger than 1½" and a bit less than 1¾".*

♥ *When making hats for babies and young children, make sure to sew down embellishments, such as the flower shown here, very securely. Use knots to finish the ends of the sewing yarn, since simple weaving may not be enough to keep little fingers from pulling the flower off.*